Travis Swann Tay

111 Places in Atlanta That You Must Not Miss

emons:

© Emons Verlag GmbH
All rights reserved
Photographs by Travis Swann Taylor, except see p. 238
Cover motif: shutterstock.com/naulicrea
Edited by Karen E. Seiger
Maps: altancicek.design, www.altancicek.de
Basic cartographical information from Openstreetmap,
OpenStreetMap-Mitwirkende, ODbL
Printing and binding: Grafisches Centrum Cuno, Calbe
Printed in Germany 2020
ISBN 978-3-7408-0747-4
First edition

Did you enjoy this guidebook? Would you like to see more?
Join us in uncovering new places around the world on:
www.111places.com

Foreword

I first moved to Atlanta to create a new life for myself. I'd lived all over the US and in Europe for more than two years, and Atlanta just seemed to make sense for me. Moving here cemented my love for big-city life, and this is where I shed my shyness with each new place I visited and with each new experience. From canoeing on the Chattahoochee River to dining at the Sun Dial, 72 stories above the city, each new adventure confirmed that I'd found home.

But 15 years later, I felt a profound need for change. So I moved to Washington, DC, started a career in corporate communications, working with the world's largest satellite communications company – a dream come true for this space geek. I visited more of the world while living in DC, and I volunteered at the Smithsonian's Natural History and Air & Space Museums (if you want to get to know a city quickly, volunteer!). However, after nine years, Atlanta beckoned. I found that I was missing Atlanta's charm, her Southern hospitality, and her smallest-big-city-you'll-ever-live-in feel.

Atlanta had grown significantly while I was away, so I started a blog, *wanderlust ATLANTA*, to refamiliarize myself with the city. I also became a docent at the Atlanta Botanical Garden. Armed with a laptop and a camera (I've had a camera since I was 10 years old), I set out to experience what was new here – and there was a lot. I fell in love with Atlanta all over again!

Fast-forward a few years, and I am still writing that blog that I was only going to do for one year – Atlanta is that much fun. There's always something new to see, do, taste, or experience. Writing and doing the photography for this book has been another dream come true. The stories on these pages have afforded me the opportunity to share my love for this city, the amazing places here, and, most importantly, the kind and hospitable people who also call Atlanta home.

Travis Swann Taylor

111 Places

1   5Church Atlanta

Dining for art lovers

5Church Atlanta is a vibrant, Midtown restaurant that features New South cuisine, and diners can enjoy the thoughtfully curated collection of art showcased there. The largest artwork is the restaurant's ceiling. It's painted black with white lettering. Owner Ayman Kamel says, "The hand-painted ceiling, which displays the text of 5th-century Sun Tzu's *The Art of War,* is a tribute to our establishment's philosophy that 'THERE IS ONLY WE.'" It's painted in large letters over the 32′ 5″ bar.

When your eyes return to room level, you'll see a gigantic coin created by Georgia native William Massey. His *Buffalo Nickel* sculpture depicting an American buffalo is created with discarded materials to symbolize the resilience of the United States, the unification of 5Church, and the ingenuity to make old things new. Artist Ishmael's painting for the restaurant, called *The Fifth Dimension*, is based on a 1925 photograph of Atlanta's Five Points and gives viewers a sense of the city's past, present, and future.

Bhakti Baxter's larger-than-life mural in the stairwell leading to the rooftop was inspired by King George II – Georgia's namesake – and his fondness for hunting stags. The mural depicts a stag and its reflection, flanked by red oak and magnolia trees, both abundant in the South. The deer appears to the viewer as if it's being hunted, while its blue reflection represents the animal's indestructible spirit waiting in a parallel dimension.

Ayman noted that the art in the restaurant is purposefully selected to contribute to the 5Church dining experience. "We refresh our art collection from time to time to give our diners a different experience. We're planning a rotating art gallery for our upstairs event room that will support local artists. They can exhibit at no cost to them. It's one of the ways we give back to the community, and it helps us feed all the senses."

Address 1197 Peachtree Street NE, Atlanta, GA 30361, +1 (404) 400-3669, www.5churchatlanta.com | Getting there Red or Gold Line to Arts Center | Hours See website for hours | Tip Catch a performance of the Atlanta Symphony Orchestra, a show at the Alliance Theatre, or visit Georgia's largest art museum, all within the Woodruff Arts Center less than one block away (1280 Peachtree Street NE, www.woodruffcenter.org).

2 _ *54 Columns*

Sol LeWitt prioritized concept and minimalism

Atlanta is an incredibly fast-growing city, which means lots of construction. In fact, some joke that our city bird should be the "Construction Crane." If you happen to notice the installation of *54 Columns* when breezing past this work of art from 1999, you could easily mistake it for an abandoned construction site. You see, this particular piece of public art is, exactly as its name suggests, made of 54 columns. They look like they are part of a construction project in its early stages because the 54 columns are naked cinder blocks. This work of art was created by artist Sol LeWitt (1928–2007), a conceptual and minimalist artist who worked primarily in paint, drawing, and "structures," a descriptive he preferred over "sculpture."

The installation is composed of 54 concrete square pillars ranging in height from 10 to 20 feet tall. They're arranged in a triangular layout, referencing the urban environment and Atlanta's skyline. The latter could be influenced by the ever popular "Best Skyline Photo" (see ch. 48) on Jackson Street Bridge only a couple of blocks away (pun intended).

Although his works are admired and loved the world over, there are people who are not fans. Perhaps some context will reveal this work of art's magnificence. LeWitt is considered to be arguably the grandfather of Conceptualism. He gave priority to the idea over the execution. Maybe you've seen *Wall Drawing #729 Irregular Color Bands* installed in the Robinson Atrium. In contrast to the unpainted columns of our Old Fourth Ward installation, *Drawing #729* is a painting with exacting, unique wide bands of color on the walls of the High's towering atrium. Once you've seen a few of LeWitt's works, you can more easily recognize his conceptual, minimalist approach to art. In fact, in 2000, *Art in America* magazine named *54 Columns* one of the top 24 public arts projects of the year.

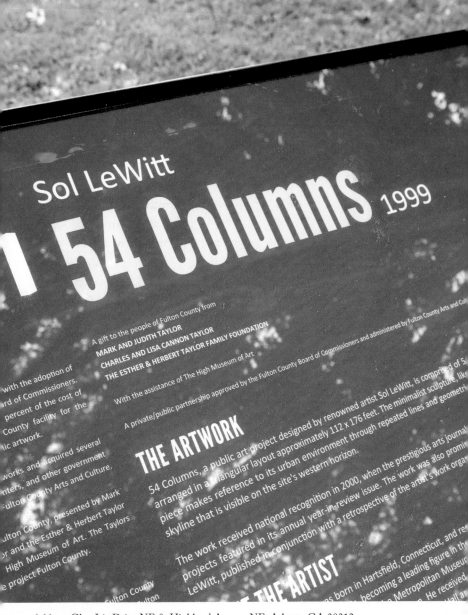

Sol LeWitt
54 Columns 1999

A gift to the people of Fulton County from
MARK AND JUDITH TAYLOR
CHARLES AND LISA CANNON TAYLOR
THE ESTHER & HERBERT TAYLOR FAMILY FOUNDATION

With the assistance of The High Museum of Art

A private/public partnership approved by the Fulton County Board of Commissioners and administered by Fulton County Arts and Cu

THE ARTWORK

54 Columns, a public art project designed by renowned artist Sol LeWitt, is comprised of 5
arranged in a triangular layout approximately 112 x 176 feet. The minimalist sculpture, like
piece makes reference to its urban environment through repeated lines and geometri
skyline that is visible on the site's western horizon.

The work received national recognition in 2000, when the prestigious arts journal
projects featured in its annual year-in-review issue. The work was also promine
LeWitt, published in conjunction with a retrospective of the artist's work orga

THE ARTIST

s born in Hartsfield, Connecticut, and re
becoming a leading figure in the
the Metropolitan Museum
He received

Address Glen Iris Drive NE & Highland Avenue NE, Atlanta, GA 30312,
www.freedompark.org/fpc/art/54-columns | **Getting there** Green Line to King
Memorial, then bus 899 to Ralph McGill Boulevard NE and Glen Iris Drive NE |
Hours Unrestricted | **Tip** See one of Atlanta's architectural marvels inside and out!
Tour Mercedes-Benz Stadium, where you'll be in awe of its purposeful design and the
unique experience it brings to visitors (1414 Andrew Young International Boulevard,
www.mercedesbenzstadium.com/stadium-tours).

3 _ 57th Fighter Group
Planes practically land on your table

You'll drive by a WWII Jeep and through Checkpoint Charlie. You'll enter the 57th Fighter Group through sandbag barrier walls. Inside, you'll see hundreds of photographs of thousands of honored American veterans from World War II. While dining, whether in the main dining room or on the spacious patio, you'll enjoy the exhilarating ambience with planes taking off and landing at Peachtree-DeKalb Airport from a runway-side vista.

The WWII P-51D Mustang airplane situated in front of the restaurant was painted in the colors of lifelong Atlanta resident Captain Robert "Punchy" Powell's plane. Punchy was a member of the 352nd Fighter Group, which completed 420 missions, destroyed 776 enemy aircraft, and produced 29 aces, logging 600,000 combat hours. The sprawling restaurant space, designed to resemble a bombed-out French farmhouse, features multiple intimate dining rooms with cozy fireplaces, an open kitchen, and two private event rooms, one adorned with Vietnam veterans' photographs. There's a large lounge with a dance floor, and a spacious patio area with fire pits and table service – the patio view is especially spectacular on evenings with a full moon. And the voice you hear in the bathroom is Prime Minister Winston Churchill's.

The 57th Fighter Group Restaurant menu features American comfort food with regional influences and a "Grand Champagne Sunday Brunch" buffet. Try the Made-to-Order Bananas Foster. And you'd be remiss if you didn't taste their famous Beer Cheese Soup. The restaurant's dance floor is packed on Friday and Saturday nights with a multi-generational, highly energetic crowd. The more seasoned dancers and the younger energetic ones blend mid-evening with music from a live DJ catering to all tastes. Originally part of a group of 52 restaurants, each named for a unique WWII fighter group and all on airfields, this is one of only six that remain.

Address 3829 Clairmont Road, Atlanta, GA 30341, +1 (770) 234-0057,
www.the57threstaurant.com | Getting there Gold Line to Chamblee, then bus 19 to
Clairmont Road and Georgian Drive | Hours See website for hours | Tip Biplane Rides
Over Atlanta, situated between the restaurant and the runway, offers biplane rides
above the Atlanta skyline, Stone Mountain, Lake Lanier, and Mercedes-Benz Stadium
(3829 Clairmont Road, www.biplaneridesoveratlanta.com).

4   191 Peachtree Tower

The chandeliers are Instagram-worthy

191 Peachtree Tower was completed in 1990, just about the time that grandeur had fallen out of fashion – again. Early critics panned its lavish beauty, and some even said that it could not possibly stand out in Atlanta's skyline. They were terribly wrong, of course. The twin-colonnade crown atop the 50-story skyscraper is among the most distinctive in the Southeastern United States. Its design is just as stunning from street level. Its soaring seven-story atrium lobby on Peachtree Street and its four-story lobby on Peachtree Center Avenue NE secure this building's distinctive, tastefully opulent, and classically elegant place among Atlanta's architectural treasures.

The Tower is recessed from Peachtree Street by its stone and glass lobby, the idea being that the space be used for civic and private events. Today, part of it is used as seating for a neighboring restaurant, and it's connected to the Ritz-Carlton on the other side.

The chandeliers in the Peachtree Street lobby are Instagram-worthy. Architects Philip Johnson and John Burgee placed four gigantic, Fabergé-esque chandeliers here, similar to the chandeliers in Grand Central Terminal in New York City. Coincidentally, those fixtures were designed by Bradford Gilbert, who designed Atlanta's Flatiron Building (see ch. 6).

The seven-story double crown sits atop two connected square towers. Slender shafts of stone and glass run the full height of the building, further enhancing the verticality of the towers and creating 12 corner offices per floor. The building is clad in flame-finished Rosa Dante granite and tinted glass. When Johnson/Burgee Architects was formed, Burgee noted that Atlanta's skyscrapers had no roofs. He changed that in 1987 with the former IBM Tower (today One Atlantic Station), which in essence was the beginning of the future of Atlanta's distinctive skyline, now filled with numerous unique roofs.

Address 191 Peachtree Street NW, Atlanta, GA 30303, www.191peachtree.com | Getting there Gold or Red Line to Peachtree Center | Hours Unrestricted | Tip You can begin the learning process of how to make your own chandelier at Janke Studios, Atlanta's first complete glass-blowing center. Schedule a "Date Night" or a class (659 Auburn Avenue NE, www.jankestudios.com).

5 __ 1895 Exposition Steps

1 park, 100 days, 6,000 exhibits, 800,000 visitors

What makes the wide stairs flanked by giant planters in Piedmont Park remarkable is that they're the only remnants in the park from the 1895 Cotton States and International Exposition.

Over the last 100 days of 1895, more than 800,000 visitors (Atlanta's population at the time was approximately 75,000) made their way to Piedmont Park from all over the world to see how the New South could contribute to the national economy and to foster positive international relationships. There were 6,000 exhibits that covered the cotton industry, food production, transportation, education, art, and electricity. Motion pictures were first introduced to the public.

Just two years earlier, the Ferris Wheel, America's answer to the Eiffel Tower, had debuted at the Columbian Exposition in Chicago. So Atlanta built their own "Phoenix" Wheel, named after the city's glorious symbol of rebirth (see ch. 73).

Most attendees had never experienced foreign cultures and were utterly fascinated by "villages" from Japan, China, Mexico, and Egypt. Every building was adorned with the American flag. There were also Native Americans in full warrior regalia.

There were seven state buildings. The Liberty Bell was on display in the Pennsylvania State Building, which received the most visitors. On Liberty Bell Day, October 9, 30,000 visitors came to see America's most recognized symbol of liberty. The Negro Building was the first exposition building in the world to showcase the accomplishments of post-slavery African Americans, and congressional funding was dependent on the exposition hosting such an exhibition.

Buffalo Bill's Wild West Show had 500 employees, including sharpshooter Annie Oakley. His contract did not specify the number of days his show would be required to run. He was there for one week and then departed as soon as the weather turned cold.

Address Piedmont Avenue NE, Atlanta, GA 30309, +1 (404) 875-7275, www.piedmontpark.org | Getting there Red or Gold Line to Arts Center, then bus 27 to Piedmont Avenue NE and Prado | Hours Daily 6am–11pm | Tip Grab a cold craft beer, a burger, sushi, and more at Park Tavern inside Piedmont Park, and enjoy it indoors or on their spacious patio (500 10th Street NE, www.parktavern.com).

6 1897 Flatiron Building

Constructed five years before NYC's Flatiron

One of the city's tallest buildings at the time of its construction in 1897, the Atlanta Flatiron Building gets its name from its elongated triangle shape that resembles an iron. The household appliance has roots back to 1st-century China, and the modern electric clothes iron was invented by Henry W. Seely of New York City. Seely filed a patent on June 6, 1882 for what he called the "electric flatiron." Atlanta's Flatiron Building was designed by Bradford Gilbert who was the supervising architect for the 1895 Cotton States and International Exposition (see ch. 5).

The 11-story Flatiron Building, Atlanta's oldest standing steel-framed skyscraper, predates New York City's more famous, 22-story Flatiron Building, which was completed five years later in 1902. Although similar in shape, their styles and architectural features are different. The Atlanta Flatiron Building boasts stunning bay windows along its Peachtree and Broad Street façades, and its location adjacent to Woodruff Park provides an exquisite setting for this architectural gem in the heart of downtown Atlanta.

According to urban historian Kenneth T. Jackson in his book *The Ku Klux Klan in the City, 1915–1930*, the Klan, after being dormant for more than 40 years, had its first office in a loft of the building. And an Imperial Kleagle also had a recruiting office there. City directories show only that he had a business office in the building, and the Klansmen had prominently displayed addresses at other locations in the city, never officially in the Flatiron Building. But Professor Jackson's research tells a different story.

Today, this beautiful and storied structure still functions as an office building. Situated next to Woodruff Park coupled with its active pedestrian traffic on Broad Street, the building garners lots of attention from passersby and is popular with photographers. This great beauty continues to withstand the test of time.

Address 84 Peachtree Street NW, Atlanta, GA 30303, +1 (470) 428-2153,
www.flatironcity.com | Getting there Gold or Red to Peachtree Center | Hours Unrestricted
from the outside only | Tip Quench your thirst in East Atlanta Village at the Flatiron Bar &
Restaurant, located in a historic Flatiron Building built in 1911 that was the East Atlanta
Banking Company. Enjoy the menu and a game of pool or darts upstairs (520 Flat Shoals
Avenue SE, www.flatironatl.com).

7 Agatha's

A deliciously fun whodunit experience

Someone has been murdered! And you'll help solve the case during a five-course meal and four acts of whodunit hilarity in which everyone plays a part. When you arrive at Agatha's: A Taste of Mystery (park in their discounted parking lot), you'll be greeted by actors from the show. They'll give you an orientation, hand you your randomly assigned role in the show, and take your entrée order. The first course is a buffet of hors d'oeuvres. There's a full cash bar in the lobby, so enjoy your favorite libation. You're not required to play a part – they're here to entertain, not embarrass – but many who decline a role often change their minds before the show starts, and for good reason: it's fun!

Once you are seated, the show begins. The shows are almost always themed around pop-culture, but don't worry – even if you don't know the theme, you're going to laugh until it hurts. Regulars or those celebrating birthdays or anniversaries are often cast in "major" roles. Some have one-liners, some sing, some make up songs. It's all good, clean, deadly fun. The first seated course is soup, followed by another act. The salad course comes with a complimentary glass of wine: Chardonnay, White Zinfandel, or Cabernet Sauvignon. Then another act. Keep in mind that the four to five actors are playing two to four different characters each, so keep up!

You get to choose from six different entrées, and then there's a scrumptious dessert. Your server, who is not one of the actors, will offer you coffee, tea, and other non-alcoholic beverages, but you can help yourself to the cash bar throughout the evening. Feel free to photograph or video your friends when they're performing their scripted roles, but wait to capture the actors until after the show, when they'll be happy to meet and take photos. Co-owners Cat and Ricky have been hosts of these killer shows for more than three decades.

Address 161 Peachtree Center Avenue NE, Atlanta, GA 30303, +1 (404) 584-2233, www.agathas.com | Getting there Gold or Red Line to Peachtree Center | Hours See website for showtimes | Tip If magic is more to your liking, you'll want to check out Atlanta Magic Night, co-produced by magician Joe M. Turner, at Red Light Cafe (553-1 Amsterdam Avenue, www.redlightcafe.com).

8 AMT Gift Shop

Zombie cookbook, anyone?

Carrie Burns and Patti Davis got together for drinks. They began to talk about how Carrie's out-of-town guests always wanted to visit movie-filming sites. Suddenly, thoughts turned to starting a business to take tourists on filming site tours, something never offered before in the burgeoning filmmaking scene in Atlanta, at least not at the level they were thinking.

In only three years, Atlanta Movie Tours (AMT) would become the youngest company ever to be nominated as "Member of the Year" by the Atlanta Convention and Visitors Bureau. In subsequent years, they would expand their offerings to 10 tours, plus custom tours, of film and TV sites in Atlanta and neighboring cities. They do offer some walking tours, but mostly they offer bus tours with multiple stops to cover a larger area. All tours offer beautiful vistas and Instagram-worthy photo ops!

They would also create the AMT Gift Shop, filled with movie and TV memorabilia. Located in Castleberry Hill on the same street where Hoke (Morgan Freeman) fixed an elevator in *Driving Miss Daisy*, and also steps from the building where Merle (Michael Rooker) was handcuffed on a rooftop in *The Walking Dead*, the shop serves as the starting point for many of their tours. It's also directly across from where the action-packed *Captain America: Civil War* was filmed. And take a selfie with a platform from *The Hunger Games: Catching Fire*.

What Georgia-filmed souvenirs will you find in the AMT Gift Shop? A myriad of items, including hats, T-shirts, and mugs from *The Walking Dead*, *Vampire Diaries*, *Stranger Things*, *Marvel*, and more fan favorites, plus Atlanta Movie Tours merchandise! And of course you'll find Lauren Wilson's *The Walking Dead: The Official Cookbook and Survival Guide*, with recipes for Carl's (Atlanta native Chandler Riggs) chocolate pudding, Carol's cookies, and Hershel's (Georgia native Scott Wilson) spaghetti.

Address 327 Nelson Street SW, Atlanta, GA 30313, +1 (855) 255-3456, www.atlantamovietours.com, info@atlantamovietours.com | Getting there Gold Line to Garnett | Hours Daily 11am–5pm | Tip In the heart of Castleberry Hill is No Mas! Cantina & Hacienda. Enjoy some great Mexican food in the cantina or on the patio, and then explore the hacienda for handmade goods, gifts, and jewelry (180 Walker Street SW, www.nomascantina.com).

9 Art at the Airport

See hundreds of works of art, coming and going

The world's busiest passenger airport for more than 20 years, Hartsfield-Jackson Atlanta International Airport offers more than flights to and from the Atlanta area. This airport has on display a world-class collection of art. The "Airport Art Program" curates art for permanent and temporary exhibitions located throughout the airport's 6.8 million square feet, and the program also manages a performing arts series. You can see art in the main terminal, on the concourses, and in the passageways!

Start in the main terminal. Find the clock tower – a popular meeting place – and you'll be within steps of several temporary and some permanent exhibitions. In the Domestic Terminal are three cases displaying the artistry of Holice McAvoy, a Washington, Georgia native. The World War II planes are not prefabricated models, but rather crafted and painted by hand. Also, in the domestic terminal is a five-panel tribute to John Lewis, US Representative from Georgia who assumed office in January 1987. Titled *John Lewis – Good Trouble*, it celebrates Lewis as a preacher, activist, public servant, and a visionary. Passing through the arrivals hall in the international terminal (Concourse F), you'll have the distinct pleasure of seeing *MAMMATUS*, a one-of-a-kind, 42-feet-long sculpture by Christopher Moulder. Made with over eight miles of nickel-plated bead chain, this magnificent work of art weighs 3,000 pounds. *MAMMATUS*, installed in 2012, was inspired by mammatocumulus clouds, typically seen after the worst of a storm has passed. Artwork has moved beyond the Airport Art Program, extending to its architecture. Its new curbside canopies – at three football fields long – are works of art. Whether coming or going, take a few extra minutes out of your busy schedule to enjoy the awe-inspiring artwork and art collections throughout our artful airport.

Address 6000 North Terminal Parkway, Atlanta, GA 30320, +1 (404) 382-2250, www.atl.com/about-atl/airport-art-program | **Getting there** Gold or Red Line to Airport | **Hours** Unrestricted | **Tip** Minutes from Buckhead and Midtown, Mason Fine Art features high-quality contemporary works by regional, national, and international artists, as well as showcasing the work of new artists (415 Plasters Avenue NE, www.masonfineartandevents.com).

10 Atlanta Brewing Company

Oldest continually operating craft brewery

Greg Kelly was planning to give his new venue a traditional English brewery feel. He traveled to England in search of equipment. He found several pine-sided vats and cold tanks, as well as a large, red malt mill that had been moved to a field during World War II in case that brewery was bombed. They were never moved back inside, and they were overgrown with weeds, abandoned. A purchase, a journey across the pond, and a complete refurbishment of those artifacts was the start of Atlanta Brewing Company (ABC), which opened in 1993. Many of those magnificent finds are still in use at the brewery today.

In its first year of production, the brewery put out 4,000 barrels and named its flagship beer Red Brick, which would later become the brewery's name. Legend has it that after Sherman burned Atlanta, the city would "rise from the ashes like a phoenix" (see ch. 73) and be rebuilt "one red brick at a time." At its former location on Williams Street in Midtown, one of the brewery's neighbors was The Vortex (see ch. 102). So the brewery began crafting The Vortex's signature Laughing Skull beer, still available today.

In 2017, a landmark law was passed, allowing breweries to sell directly to consumers. ABC proceeded to expand its taproom to 28 taps, the most of any local brewery at the time. A year later, on its 25th anniversary, the brewery reclaimed its name, Atlanta Brewing Company. They're the first in Georgia to switch from plastic six-pack rings to cardboard, a sustainability initiative to develop craft beers for the Georgia Aquarium, sales of which support ocean research and conservation.

Be sure to take a selfie under the "What Ales Ya?" neon sign, seen in the spy comedy *Keeping Up With the Joneses*. Today, brewery visitors enjoy the latest ABC craft beers and evenings of live music, trivia, and comedy, featuring some of Atlanta's funniest.

Address 2323 Defoor Hills Road NW, Atlanta, GA 30318, +1 (404) 355-5558, www.atlantabrewing.com, info@atlantabrewing.com | Getting there Red or Gold Line to Arts Center, then bus 37 to Defoor Ferry Road NW and Hills Avenue NW | Hours Wed & Thu 4–9pm, Fri 4–10pm, Sat noon–10pm, Sun 12:30–7pm | Tip Just around the corner is one of Alton Brown's favs, Hankook Taqueria, a modest Korean-fusion restaurant lauded for their bibimbap (1341 Collier Road NW, www.mytakorea.com).

11 Atlanta Roller Derby

Atlanta's only all-female roller derby

Ready for some high-energy, adrenaline-rush sporting events hosted in a historically significant locale? Atlanta Roller Derby, Atlanta's first flat-track and the city's only all-female roller derby, hosts their bouts in the Yaarab Shrine Center.

Back in the 1920s, the Shriners were building a massive headquarters, but they did not have the budget to complete it. In came movie mogul William Fox, who had a number of grand movie palaces around the country, only four of which remain today. He funded the completion of what is now the Fox Theatre, and the Shriners eventually built their own Yaarab Shrine Center, where you now can go watch exciting roller derby jams.

When Atlanta Roller Derby don their skates, visitors can choose one of two bouts or a double-bout ticket. There's entertainment in the courtyard between the auditorium where the ladies skate and the Temple's main building. There's often food available (you can BYOB) and some market vendors. If you've never seen roller derby, no worries. They frequently have players hanging around the spectator bleachers specifically to answer questions about the sport or to offer a brief tutorial. Listen for the players' totally clever names during announcements.

You'll notice that both the Fox Theatre and the Shrine Temple feature Moorish architecture, a Shriners' signature style from its beginnings in 1872. When the original Shrine Temple was designed in the 1920s, its entrance was to be on Ponce de Leon Avenue, but Fox moved it to Peachtree Street. The entrance of the "new" Yaarab Shrine Temple, construction completed in 1965 and designed by Atlanta architect A. Thomas Bradbury, indeed faces Ponce de Leon Avenue. Of note, the Shriners' Temple does not hold religious significance but is rather a meeting place. Thomas Bradbury was the architect of the Yaarab Shrine Temple and the Georgia Governor's Mansion.

Address 400 Ponce de Leon Avenue, Atlanta, GA 30308, +1 (404) 872-5818, www.atlantarollerderby.com | Getting there Gold Line to North Avenue, then bus 2 to Ponce de Leon Avenue NE and Durant Place NE | Hours See website for game schedule | Tip The Atlanta Jugglers Association holds meetings twice a week at the Little 5 Points Center for Arts & Community. These meetings are practice sessions that are open to the public and they're free (1083 Austin Avenue NE, www.atlantajugglers.org).

12 Atlanta's Canopy
What we like to call "a city in a forest"

Atlanta truly is "a city in a forest." It has the most forest-rich, densest urban canopy of any major city in the US. Over 47% of the city is covered by trees, 20% above the national average, according to Trees Atlanta.

Sustaining Atlanta's canopy requires care, time, attention, and resources. It's a continual effort – and sometimes a challenge. Trees Atlanta, a non-profit citizens' group dedicated to protecting Atlanta's urban forest through planting, conservation, and education, is perhaps the most visible of all the conservation organizations because they've planted well over 100,000 trees in every neighborhood since operations began in 1985. You'll find in our canopy an incredibly diverse collection of trees, including palm trees (yes, palm trees!) and live oaks, designated as the official Georgia State Tree in 1937.

So, where do you go to see this massive, sprawling, lush canopy? There are numerous places to get a great view of our green roof, but here are a few recommendations. Enjoy brunch and carnival games on the Roof at Ponce City Market. Look out from the peak of the tallest roller coasters at Six Flags Over Georgia. Dine at the Sundial Restaurant, Bar & View at the Westin Peachtree Plaza, 70 stories above Atlanta, or go up another level and share cocktails with friends. Go on an Atlanta Beltline Arboretum tour. Or treat yourself to dessert and a nightcap at the Polaris, a rooftop revolving restaurant at Hyatt Regency Atlanta.

The absolute best way to see Atlanta's canopy, though, is a helicopter tour. Most of the helicopter tours fly over downtown, Stone Mountain (West), Truist Park, home of the Atlanta Braves (Northwest), the King & Queen Towers in Sandy Springs (North), and Lake Lanier (Northeast). The most popular helicopter tours take off from DeKalb–Peachtree Airport (PDK) and at Lake Lanier Islands. A helicopter experience is the most exhilarating, by far.

Address Various | **Getting there** Various | **Hours** See venues for hours | **Tip** Visit Stone Mountain Park, Georgia's most popular tourist attraction, and climb to the top of Stone Mountain for one of the best views of Atlanta's canopy (1000 Robert E. Lee Boulevard, Stone Mountain, www.stonemountainpark.com).

13 Atlanta's Memorial to the Six Million

Designed and built by Holocaust survivors

Nearly 20 years after the end of the Holocaust, survivors who settled in Atlanta had no place to mourn their murdered brethren, to say Kaddish. On September 3, 1964, Eternal Life-Hemshech, Inc. (*hemshech* is a Hebrew word meaning "continuation") was formed with the plan to build Atlanta's Memorial to the Six Million, a monument that would memorialize Jewish victims of the Holocaust, 1.5 million of whom were children.

The memorial was designed by architect Benjamin Hirsch. He and four of his siblings escaped Nazi Germany when their mother put them on the Kindertransport after Kristallnacht. His parents and two youngest siblings were later murdered. The memorial, managed and maintained by Hemshech, was dedicated on April 25, 1965 at Greenwood Cemetery.

The memorial features four granite walls with openings from the four corners of the Earth. The openings become narrower, symbolizing the dwindling number of those who would survive. The six white torches are lit every year during Yom HaShoah, Holocaust Remembrance Day, in Atlanta observed on the Sunday after Passover ends. The roughness of the walls and dark shadows symbolize the Holocaust, while the torches symbolize the six million Jewish lives lost. Under the torches is a crypt that contains ashes from Dachau, the first concentration camp opened by the Nazis in 1933. There's a small grave where bars of soap made from Jewish bodies are buried.

The memorial was listed on the National Register of Historic Places on April 21, 2008. Seventy-five years after the Holocaust, there are fewer and fewer survivors. But Atlanta's Memorial to the Six Million will continue to be a place to grieve, remember, and teach.

Address 1173 Cascade Circle SW, Atlanta, GA 30311, www.eternallifehemshech.org, eternallifehemshech@gmail.com | Getting there Red or Gold Line to West End, then bus 71 to Cascade Avenue SW at Cascade Circle | Hours Daily 8am–4:45pm | Tip To learn more about Jewish life in Atlanta, visit The William Breman Jewish Heritage & Holocaust Museum, which offers speaker events, traveling exhibitions, and an educational in-depth look at the Holocaust. Benjamin Hirsch also designed the Holocaust Museum at the Center (1440 Spring Street NW, www.thebreman.org).

14 Atlantic Steel Mill
This smokestack still stands

Land that once was home to a thriving steel mill employing 2,000 people in its heyday became the nation's largest brownfield redevelopment project in the late 1990s.

Atlantic Steel Mill was founded in 1901 as Atlanta Hoop Company. It produced cotton bale ties and barrel hoops. It later became Atlanta Steel Company, and in 1915 it was renamed Atlantic Steel Company. The company flourished and expanded its product offerings. By the 1980s, domestic and international competition caused reductions in force. When it finally closed in the 1990s, it sat abandoned for a period, a gruesome eyesore. It had become a brownfield, a place with the presence or potential presence of hazardous substances, pollutants, or contaminants. Structures were demolished, and soil had to be excavated and replaced.

Today, the area is called Atlantic Station, a thriving and still growing, walkable neighborhood to live, work, and play, with more than 20 restaurants, major department stores, a theater, boutiques, skyscrapers, hotels, and its own zip code. It's home to Cirque du Soleil performances, BBQ festivals, holiday events with ice skating, and the BB&T Open, the first event in the tournament series leading up to the US Open, plus movies, concerts… there's no end to things to see and do at Atlantic Station.

But all that remains of Atlantic Steel Mill on today's 138-acre Atlantic Station is the one 60-foot-tall smokestack, a nostalgic reminder of yesteryear, eclipsed by Atlantic Station's bright future.

The Millennium Gate (see ch. 74), designed in the tradition of the classical Roman triumphal arches, is perhaps *the* icon for Atlantic Station, and it's less than half a block from the original smokestack. Unbeknownst to many passersby, the Millennium Gate houses a remarkable museum. And inside that museum is a replica of the office of a former Atlantic Steel Mill president.

Address State Street at 17th Street NW, Atlanta, GA 30363, www.atlanticstation.com/
history | Getting there Gold Line to Arts Center, then Atlantic Station Shuttle to Atlantic
Drive | Hours Unrestricted | Tip You've seen the smokestack, now explore 138 acres of
shopping, dining, and events at Atlantic Station. Built from the ground up, this nationally
acclaimed redevelopment project opened as a wholly new destination in 2005 (17th Street
NW at District Avenue NW, www.atlanticstation.com).

15 BAPS Mandir

The largest Hindu temple in the US

The BAPS Shri Swaminarayan Mandir in Metro Atlanta is the largest Hindu temple in the United States. What's fascinating about this temple, aside from its spectacular beauty inside and out, is how it was constructed. It was dedicated in August 2007 after only 17 months of construction that utilized more than 1.3 million volunteer hours. The traditional *shikhar baddh* (spired) mandir is made of three types of stone: Turkish limestone, Italian marble, and Indian pink sandstone. The more than 34,000 individual pieces were hand carved in India and then shipped in 346 containers to the United States, where they were assembled.

When you first arrive, you'll be mesmerized by the monumental mandir, with its intricate carving, gold accents, the collection of flags, the statuary within the building design, the lions… you could spend hours just exploring the exterior of the temple and its grounds. Make time to go see its reflecting pool directly in front and the impressive fountain, featuring more than a dozen ornately dressed golden elephant heads whose trunks are fountain spouts. This space is perfect for meditation, relaxation, or reflection.

This is an active temple, a place of worship, but it's also open to the general public. You can go on a self-guided tour, or groups of 10 or more can make prior arrangements for a guided tour. Visitors are asked to remove their shoes before going in. (There's a room with cubbies where you can store your shoes while you're touring the inside – just remember to wear socks.) Visitors are welcome to take photographs of the exterior of the mandir, but there is no photography or videography permitted inside, so it might be prudent to leave your camera in your vehicle before you step inside the temple.

Before you leave, stop into the book and gift shop, the sweets shop, or enjoy a vegetarian meal of Indian dishes in Shayona Café.

Address 460 Rockbridge Road NW, Lilburn, GA 30047, +1 (678) 906-2277, www.baps.org/atlanta, info.atlanta@usa.baps.org | **Getting there** By car, I-85 to to Exit 99, follow Jimmy Carter Boulevard to Rockbridge Road | **Hours** Daily 9am–6pm, see website for event schedule | **Tip** Nearby is one of the oldest homes in the area, the Wynne-Russell House, built in 1826 and on the Registry of Historic Places (4684 Wynne Russell Drive NW, Lilburn, www.wynnerussellhouse.com).

16 Besharat Gallery

National Geographic Magazine's *most famous face*

While few people could tell you who Sharbat Gula is, almost every-one knows *National Geographic Magazine*'s June 1985 cover photo, *Afghan Girl*, taken by world-renowned photographer Steve McCurry. Besharat Gallery is one of only a handful of dealers around the world authorized to sell McCurry's work and the only one in Georgia. If you've never seen McCurry's photos beyond *National Geographic* magazine covers, you're in for a treat. One gallery space features only McCurry's photography, and you might actually run into him, as he visits Atlanta from time to time.

While all one gallery, there are multiple distinct areas: the main gallery, the abstract gallery, Besharat contemporary gallery, and their outdoor sculpture garden featuring multiple large pieces. There's also a full-service frame shop with a nearly infinite number of frame choices. In the middle of the gallery is Nadia's Studio, a beautifully appointed hair salon, where the walls are covered in mirrors and, of course, art. If you're looking for a luxurious European hairdo, Nadia's is the place.

Besharat Gallery has Kristofer Laméy's remarkable *Sisters*, a three-sculpture chandelier made from blown borosilicate glass and powder-coated, aircraft grade aluminum. It's spectacular in its light-ness and elegant swirls. You'll find a collection of beautiful Persian rugs in the abstract gallery, many paired with photos or paintings of the subjects depicted in the rugs.

There are also a number of magnificent motorcycles. When you begin exploring the gallery, don't be surprised if you feel like you're in an M. C. Escher drawing. There are multiple suites on three floors. The Besharat Gallery, housed in an 1885 building in Castleberry Hill, is named for owner Massoud Besharat who is an avid collector, always keeping his Atlanta gallery – and his gallery near Paris – filled with artwork of all kinds.

Address 163-175 Peters Street SW, Atlanta, GA 30313, +1 (404) 524-4781, www.atlanta.besharatgallery.com | Getting there Red or Gold Line to Garnett | Hours By appointment only | Tip A few blocks away, you'll find Marcia Wood Gallery, which features contemporary art by exceptional young artists and internationally established masters (263 Walker Street SW, www.marciawoodgallery.com).

17 Biltmore Radio Towers

An icon since 1925, only broadcasted four years

An icon on the Atlanta skyline, the Biltmore radio towers literally tower stories above the historic Biltmore Hotel. The two towers are 312 feet and 6 inches apart at their tops. And they boast wide red letters that spell *BILTMORE* on an elongated metal pyramid. Illuminated in red neon in the evening sky, they serve as a wayfinder for locals and a wonderment to visitors. Harry James Carr (1878–1958) entered the construction business in 1894 and incorporated H.J. Carr & Co. in 1909. This was the company that built the Biltmore radio towers. The towers became part of the South's first radio station, WSB (founded 1922). They were erected atop The Atlanta Biltmore Hotel in 1925 when WSB-Radio moved to the top floor, a year after the hotel's celebrated opening in 1924. They would broadcast from here through 1956, but they ceased using the towers to transmit in 1929 because they needed more power than the towers could provide.

The $6,000,000 hotel opened with great fanfare. A train called the Atlanta Biltmore Special was chartered from New York City to bring prominent Northern hoteliers and businessmen to Atlanta for the celebrations. A dinner dance that evening was broadcast nationally over the radio, and during its opening weekend, a reported 1,000 cars made the circular sweep through the hotel's driveway. The hotel's luxurious Georgian and Imperial Ballrooms still host thousands of guests every year.

The hotel welcomed celebrities such as Franklin D. Roosevelt, Dwight D. Eisenhower, Mary Pickford, Bette Davis, and Charles Lindbergh. Known as "The South's Supreme Hotel," the Biltmore was placed on the National Register of Historic Places in 1980, and it reopened again in 1999. The radio towers still serve as beacons on the Atlanta skyline, viewable for miles, inviting visitors to Midtown. Today, you can reserve the ballrooms for your own spectacular events.

Address 817 West Peachtree Street NW, Atlanta, GA 30308 | Getting there Gold Line to North Avenue | Hours Viewable from the outside only | Tip Visit the Sun Dial Restaurant, Bar & View's observation deck, offering a 360-degree view from more than 70 floors above the city (210 Peachtree Road NW, www.sundialrestaurant.com).

18 Brave a Huey or a Cobra
Ride in helicopters that flew in Viet Nam

The Army Aviation Heritage Foundation (AAHF) & Flight Museum is a remarkable hidden gem tucked away on an airfield next to Atlanta Motor Speedway, just 30 minutes from downtown Atlanta. Not many locals know about the opportunity offered here to fly with a veteran pilot on an adrenaline-infused ride in a Vietnam War-era UH-1H "Huey" helicopter. Or for something even more intense, you can ride as a single passenger in an AH-1F Cobra helicopter. Whichever you choose, if not both, it's a small splurge starting at $85, but it promises to be an experience of a lifetime. You can also watch from the ground for free as the helicopters take off and land.

The AAHF is the only educational foundation wholly dedicated to preserving flyable US Army Aviation aircraft, which are restored to their original military specifications. It is operated by volunteers, who are often busy flying groups of kids from various organizations and other thrill-seekers. So it's a good idea to pre-purchase your tickets before heading down there to make sure you'll be able to get on a flight that day.

Whether you fly or not, you should meander through the Flight Museum, which is housed in multiple hangars. There are aircraft models, awards, plaques with historic newspaper and magazine articles, and aviation memorabilia. You can take a selfie next to any of the aircraft in the hangars – ask a staff member to help you climb inside the aircraft and even take your photo. Look for the "graveyard" in the back filled with an array of engines, wings, and fuselages.

There's also an exciting bit of theater history here. In 2016, Serenbe Playhouse, a local year-round, outdoor theatre company, was the first to produce the award-winning Broadway musical *Miss Saigon* using an actual working Huey. The aircraft flew from the museum, a 20-minute flight away, and landed during the performance every evening.

Address 506 Speedway Boulevard, Hampton, GA 30228, +1 (770) 897-0444, www.armyav.org | Getting there I-75 S, exit 235 onto Tara Boulevard, right on Speedway Boulevard | Hours See website for schedule | Tip Keep the adrenaline rush going at the Atlanta Motor Speedway, billed as "a modern motorsports palace" (1500 Tara Place, Hampton, www.atlantamotorspeedway.com).

19 Carnegie Pavilion

Last remnants of the South's first public library

The four pillars that make up the Beaux-Arts Carnegie Education Pavilion once graced the façade of the Carnegie Library (1902–1977). The Carnegie Library was replaced with the 1970s, raw concrete Central Library, an often publicly criticized design, as part of the Fulton County Library System.

Placards between these columns commemorate notable authors, and the interior floor features bronze seals of nine Atlanta-area universities and colleges. It's also a very popular backdrop for superhero and other cosplay photos during the annual Dragon Con, a convention that brings more than 70,000 visitors to town.

According to the Fulton County Library System's website, the first book checked out of the Carnegie Library in 1902 was *Alice of Old Vincennes*, a Revolutionary War novel by Maurice Thompson. Anne Nicholson Wallace was the first librarian there. She was also a key organizer of the Congress of Women Librarians in association with the 1895 Cotton States and International Exposition (see ch. 5).

One of millions of immigrants coming to the United States in the mid-19th century, Andrew Carnegie, the namesake for the Carnegie Library, immigrated from Scotland. He arrived at age 13 and began working in a button factory, later in a telegraph office, and finally on the railroads. His fortune began with investments in oil and iron companies. Then he would turn to making steel railroad ties, and his timing could not have been better.

Carnegie became one of the richest men in America, a true rags-to-riches story. He would sell his business for $450 million to J. P. Morgan, who combined Carnegie's and his own companies to create the world's first billion-dollar company, United States Steel. Carnegie spent the rest of his life being a philanthropist, ultimately giving away $350 million, including the money to build the Carnegie Library, the South's first public library.

Address Hardy Ivy Park at Peachtree Street and Baker Street, Atlanta, GA 30308 | **Getting there** Red Line to Peachtree Center | **Hours** Unrestricted | **Tip** Enjoy a libation at Pulse inside the Marriott Marquis. Hardy Ivy was one of the earliest settlers in Atlanta, years before the city was founded, actually. His log cabin was on the site of the Marquis! (265 Peachtree Center Avenue).

20 CDC Museum
Anti-contamination suit optional

The Centers for Disease Control and Prevention (CDC) Museum, a Smithsonian Affiliate Museum, will make you appreciate the work of this agency to protect public health. "CDC" has always been the acronym for the organization, but its name has changed numerous times since its inception to match its evolving mission. Founded on July 1, 1946, the organization was originally named the Communicable Disease Center and eventually changed to its present-day name in 1992. You'll learn a great deal about the CDC's history, its domestic and international efforts, and its impressive success stories as you walk through the exhibits.

The first floor of the museum features rotating temporary exhibits often covering challenging diseases, the research, and achievements in treating and oftentimes curing them. The mezzanine level hosts a collection of interactive stations, enjoyed by kids and grown-ups alike. The lower level is a comprehensive, yet succinct history of the CDC. There are many diseases that we've never had to fear or experience because of research by the CDC to create medicines and/or preventative actions. The museum chronicles many of these efforts, including the global eradication of smallpox in 1980, polio (you can see an actual iron lung capsule), legionnaires' disease, and many others. They also worked with NASA in the 1960s to create a Mobile Quarantine Facility.

You can pick up a copy of the CDC's *Morbidity and Mortality Weekly Report*, a publication that has not missed a Thursday printing deadline since its first edition in 1961. The report is used by public health officials the world over and often by journalists reporting breaking news. In June of 1981, the publication was the first to report on the first known cases of the later-named AIDS virus.

Photo ops abound here, but the best one is your chance to climb into an anti-contamination suit!

Address 1600 Clifton Road NE, Atlanta, GA 30329, +1 (404) 639-0830, www.cdc.gov/museum | **Getting there** By car, GA-10 to US-278 E/Ponce de Leon Avenue NE, turn onto Clifton Road NE | **Hours** Mon−Wed & Fri 9am−5pm, Thu 9am−7pm | **Tip** Nearby Emory Point is a mixed-use destination with excellent dining and shopping options! (855 Emory Point Drive, www.emory-point.com).

21 _ Century Flood Line
Beauty and flood mitigation in one park

At the north end of Historic Fourth Ward Park, across the street from Ponce City Market, is the Clear Creek Basin and an amphitheater, a popular gathering place for neighborhood residents and visitors. But it also serves as a storm water run-off reservoir, significantly reducing flooding in nearby sections of the Old Fourth Ward neighborhood. It does and will flood in heavy rains, but the winding walkways, artscapes, and landscapes in the basin, including indigenous plants and flowers, were specifically designed to endure high water levels. After any heavy rain, run-off water recedes, and the fun resumes.

The basin is not visible from its surrounding streets to the north and the east. You must walk up to the park to even see it, and it's quite the surprise the first time you see the expansive two-acre body of water. In the middle of the basin's pond on its south end is a fountain spraying at least 10 feet into the air, simultaneously aerating the pond water. There's another water feature at the north end of the basin that's a contemporary work of art, composed of massive vertical granite slabs and several waterfalls.

Along the granite walls of the basin, following decorative walking paths, are two flood lines marked in river rock. The lower line is the 100-year flood line, and the upper line is the 500-year flood line. A 100-year flood line is not a prediction of a flood of the same magnitude every 100 years, but rather indicates a 1% chance of the same magnitude flood in any year.

The first development on this site was in 1903 when the Ponce de Leon Amusement Park opened and where Ponce City Market is today. The amusement park offered a casino, theater, a merry-go-round, a penny arcade, two restaurants, and more. After a period of neglect and abandon, Historic Fourth Ward Park is again teeming with life and flooded with fun, festivities, and amusement.

Address 665 North Avenue NE, Atlanta, GA 30308, +1 (404) 590-7275, www.h4wpc.org, info@h4wpc.org | Getting there Gold Line to North Avenue, then bus 899 to North Avenue and Glen Iris Drive | Hours Daily 6am–11pm | Tip You can't miss Ponce City Market – it's across North Avenue, and it's one of the most lauded repurpose projects in the country. Go for a meal, drinks, shopping, and you can even rent a bike and explore the adjacent Atlanta Beltline (675 Ponce de Leon Avenue NE, www.poncecitymarket.com).

22 Coca-Cola Bottling Plant

First plant to bottle the addictive elixir in Georgia

Designated a National Historic Landmark in 1983, the Dixie Coca-Cola Bottling Company Plant is the oldest surviving building associated with the early days of Coca-Cola, or "Coke," as it's called around the world. The very first Coca-Cola bottling plant had been opened in Tennessee, but this was the first one in Georgia, home of Coca-Cola. The oddly shaped, two-story, brick Victorian building served as headquarters for the company and its plant from 1900 to 1901. There was an automated factory in the basement, where the Coca-Cola syrup was produced, and the company's offices were on the upper floors. The plant was so successful and grew so quickly that operations had to be moved to another location in under a year. They sold 16 bottling plant franchises in Georgia and then took the company to a national scale.

This building, which originally provided space for shops on the lower floor and living quarters above, represents Coca-Cola's transformation from being strictly a fountain treat prepared by a soda jerk at a counter to primarily a bottled drink sold at local groceries. Between being a Coca-Cola bottling plant and a Baptist ministries outreach, this building has served as other things to many people, including a produce market, a ladies lingerie shop, a plumbing shop, and an arts and craft shop. The upstairs portion was later used as a boarding house.

During the period of World War II, as with so many other houses in the area, the building was known as a "house of ill repute." From 1953 until 1969, Brown's TV Repair Service was on a long-term lease. In 1964, the Atlanta Baptist Association purchased the property, but they would not operate here until Mr. Brown's passing in 1969, when his estate's executors surrendered the long-term lease. Today, the 1891 building is home to Baptist Collegiate Ministries at Georgia State University.

Address 125 Edgewood Avenue SE, Atlanta, GA 30303, www.nps.gov/nr/travel/atlanta/ dix.htm | Getting there Blue Line to Georgia State | Hours Unrestricted from the outside only | Tip The Varsity, a drive-in that opened in 1928, once sold more Coca-Cola than any other restaurant in the world! Enjoy a hotdog and the onion rings there (61 North Avenue, www.thevarsity.com).

23 __ Coca-Cola Sign

A beacon to the birthplace of Coca-Cola

On Saturday, May 8, 1886, the first glass of Coca-Cola was sold for five cents at Jacob's Pharmacy in downtown Atlanta. The refreshing beverage was invented by John Pemberton, a pharmacist, in his lab nearby. Today, a 33-foot-wide, bright red neon sign in Five Points serves as a beacon for the birthplace of Coca-Cola. The sign sits atop the Olympia Building, where, in the 1840s, a wooden structure housed a general store and Atlanta's first post office. The post office was run by George Washington Collier, considered to be Atlanta's first postmaster.

Jacob's Pharmacy was situated on Marietta Street diagonally across the street from the sign, in what is today the Georgia State University-Andrew Young School of Policy Studies building. Look for the black historical marker on the sidewalk denoting the former location of the pharmacy. In the Olympia Building, designed by Ernest Daniel Ivey and Lewis Edmund Crook in 1936, was the first Tom Pitt's Soda Fountain. Such soda fountains, many sporting Coca-Cola signs, were so popular for socializing with friends that some called their gatherings, "Coca-Cola Clubs."

From 1932 to 1981, a Coca-Cola sign hung in Margaret Mitchell Square, five blocks north on Peachtree Street. That sign was a well-known landmark for downtown Atlanta, as is the current Coca-Cola sign, which has been in its current location since 2003. In 2019, the sign went dark, as it had briefly in the 1970s during the energy crisis, but this time it was for a technological upgrade. The new sign has LED lighting and a full-color, interactive digital display that allows it to be illuminated 24 hours a day.

Across the street northwest is Woodruff Park (see ch. 6 & 73), named for Coca-Cola's longest-standing leader, Robert Winship Woodruff. For more than half of the 20th century, he worked to expand the beverage into a global brand.

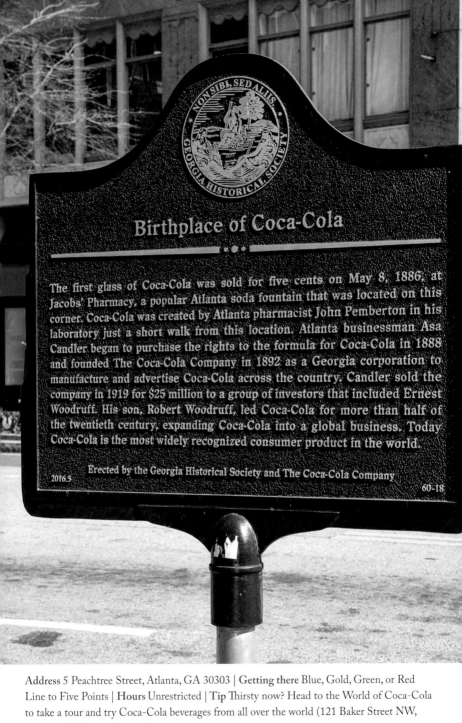

Birthplace of Coca-Cola

The first glass of Coca-Cola was sold for five cents on May 8, 1886, at Jacobs' Pharmacy, a popular Atlanta soda fountain that was located on this corner. Coca-Cola was created by Atlanta pharmacist John Pemberton in his laboratory just a short walk from this location. Atlanta businessman Asa Candler began to purchase the rights to the formula for Coca-Cola in 1888 and founded The Coca-Cola Company in 1892 as a Georgia corporation to manufacture and advertise Coca-Cola across the country. Candler sold the company in 1919 for $25 million to a group of investors that included Ernest Woodruff. His son, Robert Woodruff, led Coca-Cola for more than half of the twentieth century, expanding Coca-Cola into a global business. Today Coca-Cola is the most widely recognized consumer product in the world.

Erected by the Georgia Historical Society and The Coca-Cola Company

2016.5

60-18

Address 5 Peachtree Street, Atlanta, GA 30303 | **Getting there** Blue, Gold, Green, or Red Line to Five Points | **Hours** Unrestricted | **Tip** Thirsty now? Head to the World of Coca-Cola to take a tour and try Coca-Cola beverages from all over the world (121 Baker Street NW, www.worldofcoca-cola.com).

24__ The Cook's Warehouse

Atlanta's mothership for kitchens and cooking

Picture it: New York City, November 1993, and Mary Moore is conducting a cooking demonstration in Manhattan's largest greenmarket. The dish she's planned required a crepe pan. But she didn't have a crepe pan. A frenzied search ends with eventual success at Bridge Kitchenware, a former retail repository of every cooking utensil, pot, pan, and gadget a chef or home cook could dream of. Two years later, Atlanta had its own mothership of kitchenwares, The Cook's Warehouse. And then Moore started offering cooking classes there.

During a Labor Day Weekend at the beach in 1994, Moore's friends had asked, "What are you going to do next?" She shared her idea for a cookware treasure trove of a store. Over the next six months, she wrote a business plan, met with numerous banks, and talked with investors. The banks were a challenge. Then, a friend put Moore in touch with a small bank that granted her a loan, which her grandmother co-signed. With that loan, plus loans from three other friends, Moore was able to make her dream come true.

Today, The Cook's Warehouse lives its tagline, "Every Excuse to Cook," by offering more than 15,000 products, including kitchen gadgets, knives, appliances, luxury cookware, attire, cookbooks, local sauces and marinades, and much more. They offer more than 600 cooking classes every year by a roster of about 40 chefs, ranging from "Pastabilities" to "Date Night Cooking," international cuisines, and holiday entertaining. "Knife Skills" is their most popular class. They teach approximately 5,000 people per year. And don't be surprised if you see the likes of Sara Moulton, Nathalie Dupree, Virginia Willis, or Alton Brown.

The Cook's Warehouse has locations in Ansley Mall and Peachtree Station. For the foodie or home cook in your life, this is the perfect destination for souvenirs or just to treat yourself and maybe learn to cook something new.

Address 1544 Piedmont Avenue NE, Atlanta, GA 30324, +1 (404) 815-4993; 5001 Peachtree Boulevard, Suite 520, Atlanta, GA 30341, +1 (678) 691-8600, www.cookswarehouse.com | Getting there Varies by location | Hours Mon–Sat 10am–8pm, Sun 11am–6pm | Tip Mary is a founding member of Les Dames d'Escoffier International's Atlanta Chapter. Their biggest annual fundraiser is "Afternoon in the Country" in mid-fall at Foxhall Resort with Atlanta's best cooks and executive chefs (8000 Capps Ferry Road, Douglasville, www.ldeiatlanta.org/aitc).

25 Coyote Trading Company
Native American jewelry, art, and crafts

David Simpson, owner of Coyote Trading Company, traveled for work throughout the Southwestern US, mostly Arizona and New Mexico, and so his love for Native American culture and art began. When he moved to Atlanta in 1988, he brought his passion for Native American culture with him. He opened a shop that today offers Native American art, crafts, pottery, musical instruments, and a wide variety of handmade jewelry. His mission is to share knowledge of Native American culture and history through books, maps, historical posters and postcards, and Native American music. When you catch him at the shop, he'll regale you with stories of his travels and experiences with numerous tribes.

Dave feels a duty to preserve, promote, and protect Native American art, and he travels to the Southwest twice per year on buying trips. The store offers Native American wares from many tribes, but primarily from the Navajo, Zuni, and the Hopi people. Most of the products in the shop are labeled with their tribal origins. The store's strict "No Photography" policy is to protect the artists' designs, which are mostly one-of-a-kind. You can join Dave's email list and be one of the first to know when he's back from a trip with new merchandise. You'll find a wide selection of turquoise items, as turquoise is the most popular stone among Native American artists. Other jewelry items are made with red coral, orange and purple shells, malachite, onyx, and mother of pearl. There are also beautiful wooden flutes, rattles, and drums, as well as some CDs of Native American music.

Dave's initial attraction to Native American culture was their ability to exist in harmony with nature, to live in balance with the natural world around them. The store moved to Little Five Points in 1992, the perfect locale, according to Dave, because of the neighborhood's diverse, tolerant, and creative community.

Address 419 Moreland Avenue NE, Atlanta, GA 30307, +1 (404) 221-1512, www.coyotetrading.com | Getting there Blue or Green Line to Edgewood-Candler Park | Hours Mon–Fri noon–8pm, Sat 11am–8pm, Sun noon–6:30pm | Tip The Etowah Indian Mounds form the most intact Mississippian Culture site in the Southeast. The 54-acre site was home to several thousand Native Americans from 1000 A.D. to 1550 A.D. (813 Indian Mounds Road SE, Cartersville, www.gastateparks.org/EtowahIndianMounds).

26 Crypt of Civilization
To be opened in 8113 A.D.

Dr. Thornwell Jacobs created his own time capsule to give future archeologists insight into human civilization from 1920–1938. He called it the "Crypt of Civilization" and sealed it in 1940. It is scheduled to be opened at noon on May 28, 8113, over 6,000 years in the future.

Dr. Jacobs re-founded Oglethorpe University, which was originally started in 1835 by James Oglethorpe, the founder of the colony of Georgia. The modern cornerstone was laid in 1915, and Jacobs would serve as its president for nearly 30 years. The world learned about Jacobs' time capsule in a 1936 *Scientific American* article, which referred to it as, "America's answer to King Tut's tomb" – a mere 14 years after the discovery of the young Egyptian king's grave.

Jacobs had previously come across an ancient Egyptian calendar dating to 4241 B.C., thought at the time to be the beginning of recorded history. So, while planning his own time capsule in 1936, he doubled that year and added 4,241 to calculate the year in which his time capsule should be opened (1936 + 1936 + 4241 = 8113). Among the more than 4,000 relics in the capsule are a microfilm record of more than 800 books; models of the Egyptian pyramids, Stone Mountain, and the Eiffel Tower; recorded speeches by Franklin D. Roosevelt, Adolph Hitler, and Benito Mussolini; a quart of beer; a doughnut cutter; and a flyswatter.

The Crypt of Civilization is buried under seven feet of rock. It's encased in 30-inch walls of steel and granite from nearby Stone Mountain and is enrobed in zinc. The 20-foot-by-30-foot container (2,000 cubic feet) is filled with nitrogen gas, thought by Jacobs to help prevent or slow any decay of the Crypt's artifacts. Engraved cards were sent to the backers, guaranteeing that any descendent of a named contributor to the building and furnishing of the Crypt would be admitted to the opening ceremony in 8113.

Address 4484 Peachtree Road NE, Atlanta, GA 30319, www.crypt.oglethorpe.edu | Getting there Gold Line to Brookhaven-Oglethorpe, then bus 25 to Post Brookhaven or walk | Hours Viewable on special tours or public events only | Tip Buried outside the Atlanta History Center's northwest side, under three enormous columns from the Historic Equitable Building of 1892 (demolished in 1971), is a time capsule from 2016 that contains artifacts commemorating SunTrust Bank's 125th anniversary, to be opened on their 150th anniversary in 2041 (130 West Paces Ferry Road NW, www.atlantahistorycenter.com).

27 DeKalb Bottle House

Drive-thru or come in and browse

Dekalb Bottle House is one of the few drive-thru adult beverage stores in town. Those licenses are no longer available in Atlanta, but DeKalb Bottle House is "grandfathered" in. It also has remarkable barrel partnerships of more than 15 years, with batches of bourbon and tequila personally selected especially for only this shop. This small business, celebrating its 30th anniversary in 2020, values a sense of community and excellent customer service as much as its high-quality and diverse offerings. By the look of it, though, you wouldn't know that just inside the doors is an incredibly diverse selection of liquors, wines and bubbles, and beers – global and local – surely unmatched when compared to others of this size.

Wed in the United Kingdom, Jat and Achla Patel moved to Athens, Georgia in 1989 and then to Atlanta in 1990, when they opened DeKalb Bottle House. Jat was trained in osteopathic medicine but found his career path working in a friend's package store in Athens. Keeping up with, or even ahead of trends, around 2005 Jat developed barrel partnerships with distilleries in Kentucky. He visits, tastes, and then selects barrels that are then bottled just for the shop's customers.

Jat visits Mexico and does the same for tequila offerings. The shop will have 5 – 10 exclusive barrel offerings at any given time. They also offer craft beer from about 20 local breweries, which makes up about 40% of their beer inventory at any given time. Their wine and bubbles selections are from the most popular wine-producing countries in the world.

One of their community-building events is a biannual wine and bourbon tasting event at a neighborhood "Beach Club" in spring and fall. For a modest ticket cost, the 70 – 100 guests enjoy small bites and samples of 60 – 80 wines from around the world, all while hanging out with Jat and Achla in a casual, festive atmosphere.

Address 3111 Briarcliff Road NE, Atlanta, GA 30329, +1 (404) 636-0790, www.dekalbbottlehouse.com, info@dekalbbottlehouse.com | Getting there Gold Line to Chamblee, then bus 19 to Clairmont Road and Briarcliff Road | Hours Mon–Thu 9am–10pm, Fri & Sat 9am–11pm, Sun 12:30–7pm | Tip Go across the street to Desta Ethiopian Kitchen for some of the best Ethiopian food in the city. In a hurry? Get the vegetarian platter to go (3086 Briarcliff Road NE, www.destaethiopiankitchen.com).

28 DeKalb History Center

Learn about history older than Atlanta

DeKalb County was formed in 1822 from portions of Fayette, Henry, and Gwinnett counties. DeKalb is named after Baron Johann de Kalb, who was from Germany and aided the colonists in their fight for independence during the American Revolutionary War. The county seat, formed in 1823, is named for Stephen Decatur, a naval hero from the War of 1812. Atlanta itself would not be officially founded until 1837.

The Historic DeKalb County Courthouse, today home of the DeKalb History Center and its archives and museum, was the fourth and fifth – of six – DeKalb County courthouses. The first one, built in 1823, was a crude wooden building. The fourth one (actually the fifth one redesigned after the original fourth suffered extensive fire damage) was built by the architecture firm Golucke & Stewart. James Wingfield Golucke (1865–1907) designed about 15 courthouses in Georgia on his own. With partner George Wilson Stewart (1862–1937) he designed five Georgia courthouses and other buildings, and Stewart designed five on his own.

The DeKalb History Center, established in 1947, today manages its museum which presents numerous exhibitions, some permanent and many special exhibitions, specific to DeKalb County. They offer historic courthouse tours, neighborhood architectural walking tours, and other public activities.

A handsome, hand-colored photograph here is of William Schley Howard, who was born in the neighborhood of Kirkwood, served as a sergeant in the Spanish-American War, and was a US Representative from Georgia 1911–1919. He was a defense lawyer in the case of Leo Frank (see ch. 64). According to a 2009 article on *Pieces of Our Past*, Howard "defended more than five hundred persons accused of murder, more than anyone in the entire United States." He later stated in an interview that he never defended anyone who had pleaded guilty to murder.

Address 101 East Court Square, Decatur, GA 30030, +1 (404) 373-1088, www.dekalbhistory.org | Getting there Blue Line to Decatur | Hours Mon–Fri 10am–4pm, Sat 10am–2pm | Tip Immediately behind the DeKalb History Center is Decatur Square, where you'll find a lovely spot to enjoy a coffee, a seat to relax, and some amazing public art to admire (509 North McDonough Street).

29_ Delta Flight Museum

Walk on the wing of a Boeing 747

What began as a group of crop dusters in 1925 is today a robust airline that flies more than 180 million travelers to destinations around the world, many of them with *111 Places* guidebooks in hand. Delta Airlines had been collecting its historical archives since the 1950s, and on May 23, 1995, the Delta Air Transport Heritage Museum was launched. Forming its official corporate archives in the late 1980s, the museum opened in 1995 in two 1940s hangars. Those hangars underwent major renovations between late 2012 and mid-2014. During this time, the museum was rebranded and is now called the Delta Flight Museum.

Be sure not to miss the first Boeing 747-400 ever produced, situated near the entry gate. The forward sections of both levels remain in last-flight configuration, showing luxury like most have never seen. And don't miss your chance to take a walk on one of the airplane's wings!

The museum is presented in two groupings: Hangar 1 is "The Propeller Age," and Hangar 2 is "The Jet Age." As you walk through the blue-lit tunnel, you should hear a propeller engine transition into that of a jet engine. The new space has air conditioning and more exhibits, and it is now more accessible to the general public. The most exciting indoor exhibit is The Spirit of Delta. According to Tiffany Meng, director of operations at the museum, The Spirit of Delta was Delta's first Boeing 767-200 in the fleet, flying from 1982 to 2006. In the early to mid-1980s, Delta employees and retirees rallied together to raise $30M to buy the plane as a gift to the company. It is the only aircraft with a gold-trimmed Delta logo at the front door. It also flew in special liveries to celebrate the 1996 Atlanta Olympics and Delta's 75th anniversary in 2004. When it retired from passenger service in 2006, The Spirit of Delta had flown 70,697 hours and 34,389 trip cycles.

Address 1060 Delta Boulevard, Building B, Atlanta, GA 30354, +1 (404) 715-7886, www.deltamuseum.org, museum.delta@delta.com | Getting there Red or Gold Line to East Point, then bus 192 to North Inner Loop Road and Delta Boulevard | Hours Mon, Tue & Thu–Sat 10am–4:30pm, Sun noon–5pm | Tip Looking for more adrenaline? Head over to Porsche Experience Center Atlanta (One Porsche Drive, www.porschedriving.com/atlanta).

30__Dining on Buford Highway

Tastes from around the world on one street

Buford Highway is a 35-mile road connecting Atlanta with the city of Buford – and it's lined with international food venues. This dining around the world experience plays mostly in Asia, West Africa, and South and Central America. Enjoy culinary treats from Argentina, Bangladesh, Brazil, China, Colombia, Cuba, Dominican Republic, El Salvador, Guatemala, Korea, India, Malaysia, Mexico, Mongolia, Sichuan, Taiwan, Thailand, Venezuela, Vietnam, and many more. There are plenty of American restaurants here, too, including Southern and BBQ options. The Buford Highway corridor is one of the most ethnically diverse regions of the country and home to more than 1,000 immigrant-owned businesses.

But where to start? Tea House Formosa at 5302 Buford Highway in Atlanta is excellent for bubble tea and sweet treats. Try their guava oolong tea. Havana Sandwich Shop at 2905 Buford Highway NE in Atlanta hands down has the best Cuban sandwich in town. Enjoy a margarita on the patio at Pancho's Mexican Restaurant & Cantina at 2641 Buford Highway NE in Atlanta. In the mood for sushi? Kang Nam at 5715 Buford Highway NE in Doraville is fresh, beautiful, and plentiful. If Korean BBQ is what you're craving, there are several on Buford Highway just before and past I-285. While Atlanta does not have many 24-hour restaurants (although there are more than most would think), there are a few along Buford Highway, including Pho 24 at 4646 Buford Highway, in Chamblee.

There's even more to Buford Highway than restaurants. Plaza Fiesta (4166 Buford Highway NE) is a unique and colorful shopping experience. The Buford Highway Farmers Market (5600 Buford Highway NE) is great for the home cook. And LIPS Atlanta (3011 Buford Highway NE) offers an unforgettable drag brunch!

Address Various locations along Buford Highway NE | **Getting there** Bus, drive, or take a ride-share | **Hours** Vary by location | **Tip** Venture to Babs Midtown to enjoy a Mary-tini (think Bloody Mary with sake), named one of Atlanta's best by Thrillist! (814 Juniper Street, www.babsmidtown.com).

31 Dogwood Bench
Perch on a blossom for a beautiful skyline view

Spring brings millions, if not billions, of blossoms to Atlanta, many of which are on dogwood trees. They're perhaps more synonymous with Atlanta than Georgia's official state tree, the live oak. On the 80th anniversary of the Atlanta Dogwood Festival in 2016, the festival gifted Piedmont Park a bronze sculpture in the shape of a dogwood branch with gigantic blossoms. Sculptor Martin Dawe, founder and owner of Cherrylion Studios in West Midtown, developed and created the sculpture that also serves as a bench. He called the work descriptively *Dogwood Bench*, and it is the perfect place to take a quintessential photo of Atlanta.

The interactive sculpture is immediately to the right of the Midtown skyline reflection observation deck, with its iconic skyline views. Park-goers can sit on the bench and take photos of the Midtown skyline that are unmistakably Atlanta, especially during the Atlanta Dogwood Festival, held in the spring when dogwoods are in bloom. In fact, the festival was created in 1936 by Walter Rich, who wanted to highlight the blooming dogwood trees, and so Dogwood Bench is a perfect tribute to the founding of the event, today the third-oldest fine arts festival in the country and the oldest such event in Atlanta.

It is Lake Clara Meer that reflects the Midtown skyline so beautifully. In 1887, a small lake was created from a spring that flowed into today's visitor center. The lake was enlarged to 11.5 acres for the 1895 Cotton States and International Exposition (see ch. 5) and called Lake Clara Meer, reportedly named for Clara Annie Fritz Cheshire, the daughter of John Alexander Fritz, who owned a meat market downtown and a cattle farm on the southern edge of present-day Piedmont Park. Clara married Homer Mayson Cheshire, whose father, Napoleon Harrison Cheshire, is the namesake (with his brother Jerome) of Cheshire Bridge Road.

Address Southeast corner of Lake Clara Meer, Piedmont Park, 10th Street NE & Charles Allen Drive NE, Atlanta, GA 30309, +1 (404) 875-7275, www.piedmontpark.org | Getting there Bus 36 to 10th Street NW and Charles Allen Drive | Hours Daily 6am–11pm | Tip Explore the Atlanta Beltline Arboretum's Westside Trail and Eastside Trail, looking for signage that highlights some of the collections in the arboretum, or go on a Trees Atlanta docent-led Friday tour (www.treesatlanta.org/programs/atlanta-beltline-arboretum).

32 Donut Brunch at BeetleCat
Deliciously clever

A BeetleCat is neither a beetle nor a cat. It's a boat. Hence the nautical décor in this restaurant, or "oysterette." But donuts and seafood, you ask? Yes! You have come check out the menu for yourself.

The interiors were designed by the restaurant, bar, and residential designer Elizabeth Ingram, who later married Food Network star Alton Brown. The upstairs of the two-level dining destination showcases an oyster bar – offering about 14 kinds of oysters from all over the world – that's slightly curved around a wood-burning oven. There are Adirondack chairs on the sidewalk, and a lighthouse taller than most of your young children. Inside, the nautical appointments are as refined as they are clever. The fabric panels hovering below the ceiling are made from BeetleCat boat sails. The downstairs space is called The Den, a totally 70s retro bar, complete with paneling, string art, and burnt orange banquets and drapes.

The audio accompanying your restroom visit is also nautical in nature. You might hear theme songs from *Jaws* or *Gilligan's Island*, or late at night, it might be vintage beer commercials.

There's a full beverage menu featuring local and international libations. Their dinner menu features plates for sharing, shellfish dishes, and fin fish dishes. Their late night menu ranges from a classic cheeseburger to squid, St. Louis Ribs to conch fritters. The brunch menu highlights their clever and delicious donut offerings. Each menu contains their lobster roll, which won the 2018 *Down East Magazine* Lobster Roll World Championship in Portland, Maine!

But the donut brunch features extra clever names and prices. The Buford Highway with pork floss, salted caramel, and maple is fashioned after a sandwich at a BuHi eatery, and it's $2.85 (i.e. Atlanta's perimeter). The Irishman is made of espresso bean, chocolate, and Irish cream, and it costs $2.019 (the year the movie came out). Have a donut, enjoy brunch, and then have another donut!

Address 299 North Highland Avenue NE, Atlanta, GA 30307, +1 (678) 732-0360,
www.beetlecatatl.com | Getting there Bus 816 to Ralph McGill Boulevard NE at 828 |
Hours See website for hours and menus; donut brunch Sat & Sun 10:30am – 2:30pm | Tip
Follow the doughnut beacon that is the red neon *Hot Now* sign at Krispy Kreme, owned by
basketball legend Shaquille O'Neal. Watch the doughnuts conveyor through the cooking and
glaze dipping process (295 Ponce de Leon Avenue, www.krispykreme.com/location/atlanta).

33 Dr. Bombay's Underwater Tea Party

Where high tea supports education

The name alone promises a tea party unlike any you'd find anywhere. The walls at Dr. Bombay's Underwater Tea Party are adorned with thousands of books, dozens of tea pots, and antique bird cages. Paper parasols and origami birds hang from the ceiling. Serving up tea, multi-tiered desserts and lasting memories since 2005, this wholly eclectic place also hosts The Learning Tea, an international program that grants scholarships for young, impoverished women in Darjeeling, India.

In a cozy and quite comfortable two-room space, guests enjoy more than 70 hand-picked teas and an assortment of homemade treats. In warmer weather, there is sidewalk seating and an enclosed back patio. You have many offerings to choose from here, from a pot of tea with scones, to reservations-only high tea, to their monthly fundraising dinners, A Taste of India, which raises funds for The Learning Tea.

High tea includes your choice of teas, served with lemon, sugar, honey, and milk, and a classic tiered tray of scones, clotted cream, jam, quiche, finger sandwiches, and baked goods. The high tea experience ends with a tasting of sorbet. The monthly Taste of India benefit dinners are hosted the last Monday of the month. Diners enjoy a three-course, vegetarian-friendly, Indian meal, a raffle giveaway, and an update on the scholars in Darjeeling. This funding provides for the girls' education, dormitory-style housing, healthcare, and meals, and it also helps prevent their becoming victims of human trafficking. As members of the program, the girls are also required to participate in 10 hours of community service monthly.

Why the name "Dr. Bombay's Underwater Tea Party"? In sum-mertime, co-owner Katrell and her childhood friends would hold their breath at the local pool and enjoy their very own underwater tea parties.

Address 1645 McLendon Avenue NE, Atlanta, GA 30307, +1 (404) 474-1402, www.drbombays.com | Getting there Blue or Green Line to Edgewood-Candler Park | Hours Tue–Sun 11am–8pm; see website for high tea times | Tip Enjoy delicious recipes handed down for four generations for home-style Punjabi cuisine at Bhojanic. Their no-joking alert: "Warning: Food Contains Flavor" (3400 Around Lenox Road, Suite 201, www.bhojanic.com).

34 Ebenezer Baptist Church

Where MLK, Jr. was co-pastor

Martin Luther King, Jr.'s grandfather, A. D. Williams, moved to Atlanta in 1893 and took over the struggling Ebenezer Baptist Church. The church had 13 members at its founding in 1886, and Williams attracted 65 new members in his first year. Upon Williams' death, Martin Luther King, Sr., later known as "Daddy King," took over Ebenezer Baptist and continued growing the church. On the afternoon of Tuesday, January 15, 1929, Martin Luther King, Jr. (born Michael King, Jr.) was born in the upstairs bedroom of his childhood home (501 Auburn Avenue NE), literally around the corner from Ebenezer Baptist Church, where he would later be baptized.

In 1934, Michael, Sr. traveled to Germany and became inspired by the Protestant Reformation leader Martin Luther. As a result, King Sr. changed his own name as well as that of his five-year-old son to "Martin Luther." After giving a trial sermon to the congregation at Ebenezer at the age of 19, Martin, Jr. was ordained as a minister. Twelve years later, in 1960, Dr. Martin Luther King, Jr. became co-pastor of Ebenezer Baptist Church with his father. Martin, Jr. remained in that position until his death on Thursday, April 4, 1968, in Memphis, Tennessee. As a final farewell to his spiritual home, Dr. Martin Luther King, Jr.'s first funeral with a group of friends and family was held at Ebenezer Baptist. Honoring an earlier request by Martin, Jr., his wife Coretta Scott King arranged to play a recording of a sermon he'd given earlier in the year.

Years later, on June 30, 1974, 69-year-old Alberta Williams King, Martin Jr.'s mother, was playing the organ at a Sunday service at Ebenezer Baptist Church when Marcus Wayne Chenault, Jr. rose from the front pew, drew two pistols and began to fire shots. One of the bullets struck and killed Ms. King, who died steps from where her son had preached nonviolence.

Address 407 Auburn Avenue NE, Atlanta, GA 30312, +1 (404) 331-5190 x5046, www.nps.gov/malu/planyourvisit/ebenezer_baptist_church.htm | Getting there Bus 3 to Jackson Street NE and Old Wheat Street NE, or tram to King Historic District | Hours Daily 9am–5pm | Tip Martin Luther King, Jr.'s final resting place is at the nearby King Center, also part of the Martin Luther King, Jr. National Historic Park (449 Auburn Avenue NE, www.thekingcenter.org/plan-your-visit).

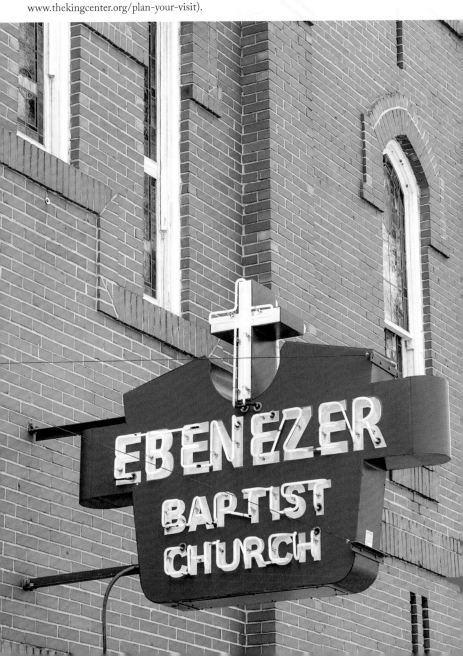

35 Emerald City Bagels

As close to New York City bagels as you can get

When you visit Emerald City Bagels to enjoy a bagel and to visit with the family owners, Deanna, the mother, and Jackie, the daughter, you may have assumed that the name Emerald City Bagels was inspired by Atlanta's once being called "The Emerald City," probably for the same reason that Seattle is called "The Emerald City," not for anything related to the mythical place in *The Wizard of Oz*, but for its lush, green landscape.

Atlanta has apparently lost that nickname – although we've tightly held on to a "City in a Forest" (see ch. 12). Deanna had named Emerald City Bagels years before she ever heard that Atlanta once carried that moniker. In the beginning, the business, which is not a store chain, but a family-owned and -operated business, began its journey in farmers' markets. They opened their bricks-and-mortar street-front business in East Atlanta Village (EAV) in January 2018, to great fanfare.

Deanna and Jackie designed the entire store themselves. It's primarily a take-out store, but there are some seats inside and a few outside if you'd like to stay for a while. They took their design inspiration from bagel shops in New York City and Los Angeles. There is a section of seats painted as a nod to the New York City subway system. There are round portholes so visitors can get a glimpse into how the goodies they're eating are made. Hanging on the wall at the end of a long corridor are two giant, golden letters that spell *OZ*.

Serendipitously, a few years before they moved into their store, they were approached by a gentleman from The Neon Company who told them that he had a green neon sign that read, "Emerald City." At the time they did not have the capital nor a place to hang it. So when they finally had a place for it, they decided they wanted that sign and went back to the man, and he still had the green sign, which has illuminated the store ever since.

SANDWICHES

LOX, CAPERS & ONIONS - 9.95

GRAVLAX, CAPERS & ONIONS - 10.95

EGG SALAD 7.95

WHITE FISH DILL SPREAD & CAVIAR 10.95

EGG ON A BAGEL 4.95
4GG CHEESE 1.50
AMERICAN
CHEDDAR
4GG MEATS 1.00-4.00
BACON
CHEESE SAUSAGE
PORK ROLL
PASTRAMI
TURKEY
HAM

TURKEY, ARUGULA & AVOCADO SANDWICH

TAVERN HAM, CHEDDAR & ARUGULA

HOT PASTRAMI - 8.95

PICKLED BEETS, DILL SPR...

VEGGIE - 7.95
CHOICE OF SPREADS
CUCUMBERS
ARUGULA
TOMATOES
PICKLED ONIONS
WATERMELON RADISH

BAGEL

BAGEL - SINGLE - 2.00
BAKER'S DOZEN - 24.00
BAGEL W/CC SPREAD 3.50 AND UP

.50 EACH
PICKLE SLICES
WHITE/MELON RADISH
PICKLED ONIONS

ADD-ONS
PICKLE SLICES - BACON 2.00
LED BEETS
R CAVIAR 4.00

SPREADS

CREAM CHEESE SINGLE

SPREAD FLAV
PLAIN
GARLIC/HERB
VEGGIE
CINNAMON RAISIN
DILL
GREEN ONIO
BLUEBERRY

EAM 3.50
CHOCOLATE
NILLA

MOKED SALMON   CREAM CHEESE   BA

Address 1257A Glenwood Avenue SE, Atlanta, GA 30316, +1 (404) 343-3758, www.emeraldcitybagels.com | Getting there Bus 4, 32, or 74 to to Moreland Avenue and Sanders Avenue NE | Hours Mon – Fri 6am – 3pm, Sat & Sun 7am – 3pm | Tip Now that you've had the best bagel in town, head over to Alon's Bakery & Market for the best New York-style cheesecake, and so much more (1394 North Highland Avenue, www.alons.com).

36 Erskine Memorial Fountain

Atlanta's oldest public fountain

The Erskine Memorial Fountain, Atlanta's first public fountain, was gifted to the City of Atlanta by Ruby Ward in memory of her father John Erskine, who had been appointed as a Federal judge by President Andrew Johnson. Erskine had wanted to make the gift himself but died before he could. So Ruby commissioned memorial sculptor John Massey Rhind, well-known for his statue of Crawford W. Long, the physician who discovered the use of sulphuric ether as an anesthetic in surgery, that stands in the National Statuary Hall Collection in the US Capitol. The fountain was dedicated on Saturday, May 2, 1896, in a ceremony that drew 1,500 citizens. Atlanta mayor Porter King gave a speech, citing the responsibility of municipal government to care for the fountain. Perhaps there were no municipal government representatives present because the fountain fell into disrepair and suffered vandalism. It was moved to Grant Park in 1912, where it had sat for over 100 years, wholly neglected.

The fountain originally stood at Peachtree Street and West Peachtree Street, in what is Hardy Ivy Park today (see ch. 87). The accompanying bench is made of Georgia marble. On the inside top of the semicircular bench are carved medallions of the 12 signs of the zodiac. The original fountain had dippers on chains hanging from it, as the fountain offered drinking water. Many pieces were stolen over the years. On Friday, July 12, 1912, an article in *The Atlanta Constitution* titled "An Insult to Civic Decency" slammed local government for not heeding the mayoral charge.

Happily, the Friends of Erskine Fountain and Grant Park Conservancy are now working diligently to repair and restore the fountain to its original working order and the bench to its former glory. They are also restoring the landscaping and the overlook behind it.

Address Grant Park, Cherokee Avenue at Ormond Street, Atlanta, GA 30308, www.friendsoferskinegp.org, info@friendsoferskinegp.org | Getting there Bus 832 to Cherokee Avenue and Ormond Street | Hours Unrestricted | Tip A few blocks north on Cherokee Avenue is the 1927 Milledge Fountain, near the Grant Park Farmers Market. It had been in gross disrepair, and water had not flowed since the 1950s, but it was recently restored (Cherokee Avenue SE and Milledge Avenue SE, www.gpconservancy.org).

37___Fernbank Observatory

A romantic, cheap date under the stars and planets

The Fernbank Science Center, not to be confused with the Fernbank Museum of Natural History although in the same neighborhood, is part of the DeKalb County Public School System. It has a planetarium – with a nominal entry fee – and an observatory open to the public for free on certain evenings. It has the makings for a lovely, stellar, inexpensive yet wholly romantic date. Take your sweetie on a journey through time and celestial events and then show them the moon, the stars, and perhaps even Jupiter.

The Jim Cherry Memorial Planetarium is 70 feet in diameter, making it one of the largest in the United States. The planetarium offers a wide range of programs, including animated space adventures and documentaries on space exploration. Planetarium programming runs throughout the day and late on Thursdays and Fridays so that guests can see a planetarium show before enjoying the observatory.

Free public observations are offered every Thursday and Friday evening from 9pm (or dark) until 10:30pm, weather permitting, and a professional astronomer is on hand to position the telescope and answer questions. You and your date can experience all three for under $15. Fernbank Science Center – where you'll see a real Apollo 6 Command Module – is free, as is parking and the observatory. The planetarium show is only $7 ($5 for kids). You might feel guilty for spending so little for so much, but that'll pass as quickly as a shooting star.

The Dr. Ralph L. Buice, Jr. Observatory houses a 36-inch Cassegrain reflector beneath a 30-foot dome, making it the largest telescope in the southeastern United States. Dr. Buice worked with Fernbank Science Center and DeKalb County Schools as a chemistry instructor for 39 years. Upon Dr. Buice's passing in 2010, the Georgia House of Representatives issued a resolution honoring his life and public service to science and education.

Address 156 Heaton Park Drive, Atlanta, GA 30307, +1 (678) 874-7102, www.fernbank.edu/planetarium.htm | Getting there By car, Ponce de Leon Avenue NE to Artwood Road NE to destination | Hours Mon–Wed noon–5pm, Thu & Fri 10am–9pm, Sat 10am–5pm | Tip You're an eight-minute drive to downtown Decatur, one of the hottest restaurant scenes in Metro Atlanta. Choose from fast-casual, to hip and trendy, to fine dining (www.visitdecaturgeorgia.com/visit/page/all-restaurants).

38 Fiddlin' John Carson

Final resting place of the origin of country music

Many know that Atlanta is the world capital of hip-hop and its most popular derivative trap music. However, few know that the country music genre got its start in Atlanta.

Yes, Nashville eventually became the world capital of country music, but it was New York record producer and talent scout Ralph Peer who ventured to Atlanta while working for Okeh Records, and found Fiddlin' John Carson (1868–1949), frequent winner of Old-Time Fiddlers' Conventions. It was 1923 when Peer recorded "Little Log Cabin in the Lane" and "The Old Hen Cackled and the Rooster's Going to Crow." Peer didn't expect roaring success and sent only 500 pressings back to the South. The record eventually sold more than half a million copies nationwide. As producers recognized the significant marketing potential of "hillbilly" or "old-time" music, the country music genre was born.

Those recordings were made at 152 Nassau Street, behind SkyView Atlanta and The Tabernacle. Preservationist, architect, and downtown resident Kyle Kessler tried for two years to save it, but even after valiant efforts, the historic building met its demise. The most we can hope for now is a historical marker at a planned Margaritaville-themed hotel, timeshare rental, and restaurant in a nod to Jimmy Buffett's 1977 hit song. Historian James Cobb links Carson's song, "The Ballad of Little Mary Phagan," performed on court steps, to the anti-Semitism that led to the 1913 Leo Frank lynching (see ch. 64).

Carson, who won "Champion Fiddler of Georgia" seven times between 1914 and 1922 and performed radio shows, is buried at Sylvester Cemetery, east of downtown. The cemetery is named for a 16-year-old boy, Sylvester Terry, who died in 1872. He was buried in the family plot at Terry Cemetery, later renamed Sylvester Cemetery. Founded in the early 1800s, today its nine acres have been undergoing restoration through a recently created foundation.

Address 2073 Braeburn Circle SE, Atlanta, GA 30316, +1 (404) 210-7312, www.sylvestercemetery.org, info@sylvestercemetery.org | Getting there Bus 74 to Flat Shoals Road SE and Clifton Road SE | Hours Contact for tour information | Tip Ralph Peer also recorded Morehouse College Quartet. Nearly 100 years later, Morehouse has vibrant music programs, many of their events open to the public (830 Westview Drive SW, www.morehouse.edu/academics/music/specialprograms.html).

39 _ Freedom Farmers Market

Have you thanked a farmer lately?

On opening day in 2014, in the parking lot of the Jimmy Carter Presidential Library and Museum, Freedom Farmers Market at the Carter Center welcomed more than 3,000 visitors. It was a huge success, to say the least. Part of that success is attributable to the philosophy of the three founding farms, Riverview Farms, Moore Farms + Friends, and Woodland Gardens. From the beginning, the market has maintained 70% of its vendor spaces for farmers, and those farmers offer "fresh organic and naturally grown produce, sustainably raised meats, farm fresh cured meats, cheese, yogurt, butter, fresh organic milk, nut milks, farm fresh eggs, handmade preserves and pickles, handmade pasta, herbal teas and vinegars, baked goods, fresh coffee, and much more!"

Market manager Holly Hollingsworth has been in the industry since 2000, previously managing Farm Mobile, a mobile farmers' market, for Riverview Farms, one of the founders of Freedom Farmers Market. Many market days are a celebration of in-season fruits and vegetables. Market-goers will enjoy Strawberry Day, Corn Day, and Peach Day, to name a few. There are special days dedicated to preparing traditional holiday meals, too.

They offer a bike valet, so you can leave your bike in safe hands while you shop. There's a kids' tent to keep the youngest ones entertained; there's live music every market day; and there's a pop-up chef selling hot-prepared foods, a huge perk in the colder months. There's also a community table, where nonprofits share their missions, ranging from saving the bees to soil health to feeding the hungry.

Within the 30% of non-farmer vendors, many of whom make their own products with ingredients from market farmers, you'll find coffee, bakeries, doggie treats, jams, pickled produce, fresh flowers, and local cheeses, and they have communal tables where you can enjoy and share your farmers' market goodies.

Address 453 Freedom Parkway NE, Atlanta, GA 30307, www.freedomfarmersmkt.org, freedomfarmersmkt@gmail.com | **Getting there** Bus 816 to John Lewis Freedom Parkway NE and Ralph McGill Boulevard NE | **Hours** Mar–Dec Sat 9am–1pm, Jan–Feb 9am–noon | **Tip** Explore Freedom Park, Atlanta's longest linear park, through its more than 200 acres connecting numerous neighborhoods, as well as the Martin Luther King, Jr. National Historic Site (ch. 58) and the Jimmy Carter Presidential Library and Museum (ch. 76).

40 From One Hundred to One

Now there's only one passenger train to Atlanta

It's no secret that Atlanta was built on railroad business. In fact, the settlement where the Georgia General Assembly decided to terminate the Western and Atlantic Railroad in 1836 was first called "Terminus." The following year, a stake was driven into the ground to mark where the railroad would terminate. Later, the Atlanta Zero Milepost would be planted to mark the location, where it would stand for more than 170 years. Housed in a train depot slated to be demolished, in 2018 it was relocated to the Atlanta History Center, where it's on display next to one of the two engines that was part of the Great Locomotive Chase of 1862 during the US Civil War.

It would be 1871 before Atlanta's railroads recovered from the war, its wooden depots having been burned by Sherman. By 1900, the now too-small depot was serving 100 trains daily. In 1903, Samuel Spencer, president of Southern Railway, officially announced their plans to build the great Terminal Station. The station was to feature 10 platform tracks, 60,000 square feet of ground space, and an additional 120,000 square feet of office space. The designs were completed by renowned Washington, DC architect P. Thornton Marye (see ch. 79). Atlanta has seen many grand train depots come and go, at one point having 10 railroads serving up to 30,000 passengers daily. Automobiles, trolleys, and buses ushered in the quick decline of passenger train service.

While many know that Amtrak's Peachtree Station, with service between New Orleans and New York, is Atlanta's only passenger station, many are unaware that it was designed by renowned architect Neel Reid (1885–1926) and that construction on the station was completed more than 100 years ago in 1918. It initially served eight trains, but now only one.

Address 1688 Peachtree Street NW, Atlanta, GA 30309, www.amtrak.com/stations/atl | Getting there Bus 110 to Peachtree Street NE and Deering Road | Hours Daily 7am–9:30pm | Tip Enjoy the Atlanta Beltline, created from former railroad pathways. When complete, it will be a complete circle through Atlanta connecting more than 40 communities (www.beltline.org).

41 Golf Legend Bobby Jones

Bring a golf ball to honor one of the greats

Robert Tyre "Bobby" Jones, Jr.'s final resting place in Oakland Cemetery is perpetually adorned with golf balls – thousands have been left over the years. Some visitors leave them for golfing luck, and some to pay their respects and to honor his memory. In 1930, Bobby was the first to complete a golf Grand Slam by winning in a single year the four major tournaments of the time: the British Open, the US Open, and the British and US amateur championships.

Considered by most golf enthusiasts to be the greatest golfer of his time, Bobby Jones always competed as an amateur. He also never accepted the cash award that came with his wins. And his record Grand Slam was not matched until 1973, two years after he passed away, when Jack Nicklaus won a career Grand Slam. The closest any other golfer has come was when Tiger Woods won the top four championships in a row, albeit not in the same season.

Bobby learned to play golf at East Lake Golf Club, then called the Atlanta Athletic Club, winning his first tournament at six years old and becoming the club's junior champion at nine. Bobby's tournament golfing career, 1923 – 1930, came to an end after his Grand Slam. He was only 28 years old. He became a practicing lawyer in Atlanta, and in 1934, he was instrumental in founding the Augusta National Golf Club. He designed the golf course which hosts the Masters Tournament today.

Bobby Jones was born in the L.P. Grant Mansion in 1902, headquarters of the Atlanta Preservation Center since 2002. The three-story Italianate mansion was built in 1856 by Grant, who had moved to Atlanta from Maine. Railroad magnate-turned-philanthropist, Lemuel Pratt Grant gifted the city of Atlanta 100 acres for Grant Park. The mansion is a four-minute drive from Bobby's final resting place with his high school sweetheart and wife at Historic Oakland Cemetery, the mansion also located in Grant Park.

Address 248 Oakland Avenue SE, Atlanta, GA 30312, +1 (404) 688-2107, www.oaklandcemetery.com, info@oaklandcemetery.com | **Getting there** Blue or Green Line to King Memorial | **Hours** Mon–Fri 9am–5pm, Sat & Sun 9am–8pm (10am–4pm during winter weekends) | **Tip** Tee off at one of Atlanta's newest golf courses, named for the legend himself, Bobby Jones Golf Course, featuring a unique reversible course (2205 Northside Drive NW, www.bobbyjonesgc.com).

42__ Gravity Monument
Chasing gravity lifted physics

Of all the things we understand about the universe, gravity itself still holds mysteries. Gravity Research Foundation founder Roger W. Babson (1875–1967), a Massachusetts Institute of Technology graduate and founder of Babson College, dedicated his later years to defeating and controlling gravity, in large part fueled by the loss of his older sister, who drowned in childhood. Babson said of the incident, "She was unable to fight gravity, which came up and seized her like a dragon and brought her to the bottom." His grandson would also drown in 1947.

Babson would pen an essay entitled, "Gravity – Our Enemy No. 1." He sought the counsel of colleague George Rideout, who recommended a program that encouraged study in the field of gravity, and thus the Gravity Research Foundation was organized on January 19, 1949. The Foundation solicited academic essays about gravity, and the first awards for the best essays were distributed in December 1949. The foundation's existence would indirectly shape careers and influence great discoveries in the field of gravitational forces.

In the 1960s, through Babson's great wealth – he'd become a millionaire as an economist, applying what he knew of Newton's Law of Gravity to the stock market – the foundation gave grants to universities, along with "headstone" monuments. Emory University received one with a $5,000 grant for the physics department. It is made of Etowah Cherokee pink marble and reads, *This monument has been erected 1962 by the Gravity Research Foundation, New Boston, New Hampshire, Roger W. Babson, Founder. It is to remind students of the blessings forthcoming when science determines what gravity is, how it works, and how it may be controlled.*

The Gravity Research Foundation essay contests continue to this day. Among the winners are theoretical physicist Bryce DeWitt DeWitt and Nobel Laureates George Smoot and Stephen Hawking.

Address Behind the Mathematics & Science Center, 400 Dowman Drive, Atlanta, GA 30322, www.emoryhistory.emory.edu/facts-figures/places/landmarks/gravity.html | Getting there Bus 36 to N Decatur Road NE at Dowman Drive NE | Hours Unrestricted | Tip …*Dooley Goes on Forever* is a stainless steel and bronze statue by Matthew Gray Palmer of skeletal Lord Dooley, Emory's ethereal and whimsical mascot, the "Lord of Misrule" (1557 Dickey Drive near the Anthropology Building, www.emory.edu/home/about/history/dooley.html).

THIS MONUMENT HAS BEEN
ERECTED 1963 BY THE
GRAVITY RESEARCH FOUNDATION
NEW BOSTON NEW HAMPSHIRE
ROGER W. BABSON FOUNDER

IT IS TO REMIND STUDENTS
OF THE BLESSINGS FORTHCOMING
WHEN SCIENCE DETERMINES
WHAT GRAVITY IS HOW IT WORKS
AND HOW IT MAY BE CONTROLLED

43 Hank Aaron's Record

Where Aaron broke Babe Ruth's home run record

It was mere steps from this Pollard Boulevard address where, according to the Baseball Hall of Fame, as Henry "Hank" Aaron swung that historic swing, Atlanta Braves broadcaster Milo Hamilton, announced, "Here's the pitch by Downing. Swinging. Here's a drive into left center field. That ball is gonna be... outta here! It's gone! It's 715! There's a new home run champion of all time, and it's Henry Aaron."

The sold-out, record-setting crowd of 53,775 at Atlanta-Fulton County Stadium exploded into applause. That historic day was Monday, April 8, 1974. Twenty years earlier, in 1954, Aaron hit a home run in his first at-bat after joining the Milwaukee Braves. He was with the Braves 21 years, 12 in Milwaukee and 9 in Atlanta, rounding out his 23 years at bat. "Hammerin' Hank" would hit a career 755 home runs and he held baseball's career record for most runs batted in at 2,297. Later, he became one of baseball's first African-American executives, with the Atlanta Braves.

The Milwaukee Braves won the 1957 World Series against the New York Yankees with Hank Aaron hitting three of the eight home runs in the seven-game series that the Braves won 4-3. The team moved to the South and became Atlanta Braves in 1966, when Atlanta officially entered Major League Baseball.

The Atlanta-Fulton County Stadium was razed and became a parking lot – marked with an outline of the now-historic field – for the Atlanta Braves, who would play in the adjacent 1996 Olympic Stadium-turned-baseball field. Today, that field is Georgia State University's football field. It's reported that Georgia State University has plans to map a new baseball field on the same one where Aaron made his home run world record. You can go see the "Hank Aaron Wall," the section of wall that Aaron's 715th flew over, memorialized in the lot. It will be preserved if Georgia State University builds their baseball stadium.

Address 640 Pollard Boulevard SW, Atlanta, GA 30312 | Getting there Bus 832 to Pollard Boulevard and Ralph D. Abernathy Boulevard | Hours Unrestricted | Tip Around the corner, Summerhill's Georgia Avenue has seen significant growth in recent years with the addition of numerous businesses, including Wood's Chapel BBQ (85 Georgia Avenue SE, www.summerhillatl.com/georgia-avenue).

44 Harry Houdini
Harry played Atlanta nearly 100 years ago

Harry Houdini, Vaudeville's great illusion act, was so long ago that we rarely hear about it at all in Atlanta. But that wasn't the case 100 years ago. Rarely making appearances in the Deep South, Houdini's first visit to Atlanta (and there weren't many) was a New Year's Day celebration at the Forsyth Theatre at Forsyth and Luckie Streets. He was billed as, "The Marvel of the Old and New World," and often advertised as "The Originator of Handcuff Tricks" and "The Handcuff King."

Forsyth Theatre opened on April 11, 1910, designed by architect A. Ten Eyck Brown. The theatre, housed in the Forsyth Building, was purely a variety venue and the home of "Keith's Vaudeville." The 1,200-seat theatre offered strictly vaudeville entertainment for its first seven years, after which it started showing movies, becoming one of Atlanta's more popular movie theaters. Saturdays at 11am were children's shows with singing and dancing. Following a period of decline, the theatre and the Forsyth Building were razed and turned into a parking lot near the intersection where Georgia State University's Rialto Center for the Arts stands today.

Harry Houdini visited Atlanta again on Thursday, March 13, 1924, at the Wimbish House, affectionately known as the "Old Lady of Peachtree," when he was the guest speaker at the Atlanta Woman's Club. He discussed his efforts to debunk fraudulent mediums in an illustrated lecture, "Can the Living Communicate with the Dead?" The Atlanta Woman's Club was organized November 11, 1895, and Wimbish House has been their home since 1920.

Although there's no marker of any kind, it was merely steps from here, at Peachtree and 13th Streets, where *Gone With the Wind* author Margaret Mitchell was hit by a speeding vehicle on August 11, 1949. She died five days later at Grady Hospital. Harry Houdini died from a ruptured appendix in October 1926.

Address 1150 Peachtree Street NE, Atlanta, GA 30309, +1 (404) 870-8833, www.thewimbishhouse.com | Getting there Bus 40 to Peachtree Street and 14th Street NE | Hours Unrestricted from the outside only; annual tours with the Atlanta Preservation Center | Tip A few blocks south, visit the Margaret Mitchell House, where Mitchell wrote the vast majority of *Gone With the Wind* (979 Crescent Avenue NE, www.atlantahistorycenter.com/explore/destinations/margaret-mitchell-house).

45 Herndon Home

From slavery to millionaire riches

Born into slavery on June 26, 1858, Alonzo Franklin Herndon would become one of Atlanta's wealthiest citizens and the city's first African-American millionaire. After emancipation in 1863, when Herndon was very young, he and his mother became sharecroppers – his father was his mother's white owner. At 20 years old, Herndon left the farm and moved to Jonesboro, where he opened his first business, a barbershop. He later moved to Atlanta, where he opened three barbershops, including the flagship Crystal Palace at 66 Peachtree Street downtown. It was adorned with chandeliers and beveled glass windows, and Herndon employed 23 barbers. Herndon took the money he made from the barbershops and invested in real estate, acquiring more than 100 properties. He made his greatest financial success in 1905 when he started what is today known as the Atlanta Life Insurance Company.

Herndon's home, which is now a museum, was primarily designed by his first wife Adrienne McNeil (m. 1893). She was in theater and one of the first three African-American teachers at Atlanta University. With theater in her heart, she designed the 15-room Beaux Arts home, perched atop Diamond Hill, one of the highest elevations in Atlanta, with a dressing room and a rooftop theater. Only a few months later, Adrienne passed away in 1910. Their son Norris Herndon would go on to bring even greater success to the family business. When Norris passed away in 1977, the family fortune went to the Alonzo F. and Norris B. Herndon Foundation, Inc., which cares for the home and continues the family's philanthropic mission. In 2000, Herndon Home was designated a National Historic Landmark.

Multi-Grammy and MTV VMA Award winner Songwriters Hall of Famer, pop icon, rapper, and celebrated innovator, Missy Elliott chose Herndon Home as a backdrop in her 2019 music video for her hit song "Throw It Back."

Address 587 University Place NW, Atlanta, GA 30314, +1 (404) 581-9813, www.herndonhome.org, contacts@company.com | Getting there Blue or Green Line to Vine City | Hours Tue & Thu 10am–4pm or schedule a tour | Tip Hungry for some true Southern, original recipe home cooking? In adjacent Castleberry Hill, Old Lady Gang restaurant, featured on *Housewives of Atlanta*, cooks up shrimp & grits, deep fried whipped deviled eggs, peach cobbler bread pudding, and more (177 Peters Street SW, www.oldladygang.com).

46___The Hoo-Hoo Monument

A labor of lumber love

The International Concatenated Order of Hoo-Hoo was founded in 1892 and is still active worldwide. There is no current chapter in the city, but on December 15, 1926, the Hoo-Hoo Club Nº1 of Atlanta erected a monument in Piedmont Park, marking the spot near the Park Drive entrance where they had planted some dogwood trees. Ten years later, the president of Rich's Department Store, Walter Rich, established the Annual Atlanta Dogwood Festival. Rich, in addition to being a highly successful businessman, was also a huge fan of gardening and the outdoors. His founding the festival was a way to "celebrate the beautiful spring season in Atlanta," according to Jeff Clemmons, author of *Rich's: A Southern Institution*. But who exactly were the Hoo-Hoo?

The Hoo-Hoo were "born" on January 21, 1892, in the parlor of Hotel Hall in Gurdon, Arkansas, organized by five men in the lumber industry who had been marooned due to train delays. The organization came together a month later at a convention in Kansas City. The founders looked to Ancient Egypt for titles, customs, and ritualistic ideas. They chose the black cat as the order's symbol, pictorially its tail curled to form a "9" in reference to the mythical number of lives of a cat, to protect members from bad luck. They hold their annual meetings on September 9 at 9:09pm. Their single aim? "To foster the health, happiness, and long life of its members."

The word "Hoo-Hoo" was coined by one of its founders to describe a peculiar tuft of hair, greased and twisted to a point, atop the otherwise bald head of a mutual colleague. The word "concatenate" means "to unite." That it has "cat" in it perhaps played a role in the lumber fraternity's name. There were no local clubs, only the national organization which met once a year. In 1920, Atlanta, Georgia became the first Hoo-Hoo Club, thus "Club Nº1" on the Hoo-Hoo Trees monument.

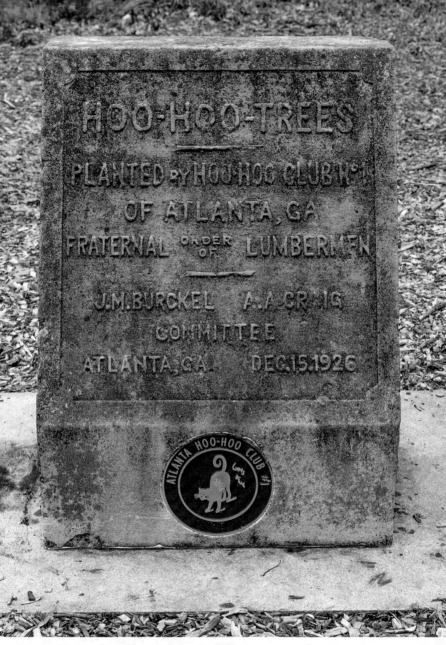

HOO-HOO-TREES

PLANTED by HOO HOO CLUB N°1
OF ATLANTA, GA
FRATERNAL ORDER OF LUMBERMEN

J.M.BURCKEL   A.A.CRAIG
COMMITTEE
ATLANTA,GA.   DEC.15.1926

ATLANTA HOO-HOO CLUB

Address 505-519 Park Drive NE, Atlanta, GA 30306, www.piedmontpark.org/
sightseeing-and-tours | Getting there Bus 809 to Monroe Drive and Park Drive |
Hours Daily 6am–11pm | Tip Panola Mountain State Park, one of Georgia's State
Parks, is only 25 minutes from downtown Atlanta (2620 Highway 155 SW, Stockbridge,
www.gastateparks.org/panolamountain).

47 Horizon Theatre Company

Where you get to meet and greet the cast and crew

Horizon Theatre Company, a professional theater nestled between historic Inman Park and eclectic Little Five Points, offers a unique theater-going experience on numerous counts. About two weeks before a production begins, Horizon opens its doors for a "Sneak Peek." They provide snacks, the concession stand is open, and tickets are free, but reserve your tickets online so that you're sure to get a seat. During the sneak peek you get to meet the cast of the show, as well as the crew, including the director, stage manager, and the scenic, lighting, sound, and music designers. Still in rehearsal and the set mid-construction, the cast will perform several acts from the play. Audience members get to ask questions of the cast and crew. These sneak peeks are a wonderful introduction to the full performance, enhancing the experience.

In a rare opportunity to engage with and get to know Atlanta's theater community, after each full performance during a show's run, cast members remain on stage and invite audience members to the stage to chat and take photos with them. The theater company's mission, accomplished through its plays and expansive programming, is "To connect people, inspire hope, and promote positive change through the stories of our times."

Horizon produces five main-stage shows per year, plus two holiday shows, one for kids and one for adults. All are contemporary and have never been seen in Atlanta, and often a regional premiere. Some are Tony Award-winning shows, and others are original Atlanta stories, such as "Waffle Palace," a show inspired by real Waffle House stories, and "Freed Spirits," a show set in Oakland Cemetery around the 2008 tornado! The 172-seat theater is delightfully intimate. Housed in a 1917 school, the theater's lobby displays information about the cast and show and often has an interactive display. Some say the shows on stage rival Broadway!

Address 1083 Austin Avenue, Atlanta, GA 30307, +1 (404) 584-7450, www.horizontheatre.com, info@horizontheatre.com | Getting there Blue or Green Line to Inman Park-Reynoldstown | Hours See website for show schedule | Tip A multitude of dining options near the theater, many within walking distance, includes The Wrecking Bar Brewpub (292 Moreland Avenue, www.wreckingbarbrewpub.com).

48__Jackson Street Bridge
Best skyline view and photo

Fans of AMC's *The Walking Dead* will recognize this vista immediately. Picture it: a skyline view of Atlanta, outbound traffic bumper-to-bumper and silent and… dead. The inbound lane features only Rick Grimes riding horseback into post-zombie-apocalypse Atlanta looking for his family. This is *the* skyline photo to take with your own family and friends when visiting our beautiful pre-zombie-apocalypse metropolis.

Some of the skyscrapers you'll see from here, left to right, include Georgia's Own Credit Union, known as the Equitable Building for 50 years prior to 2019 (100 Peachtree). It features the first digital building-top signage in Atlanta. Immediately to its right, the pink marble "steps" building (133 Peachtree Street) is the Georgia-Pacific Tower, built on the site of the former Loew's Grand Theatre, where *Gone With the Wind* premiered in 1939. The distinct double-crown pediment atop 191 Peachtree Tower hints of the opulence inside, including four Beaux Arts chandeliers in its lobby, reminiscent of the chandeliers in NYC's Grand Central Terminal (see ch. 4).

The tall, cylindrical building is the Westin Peachtree Plaza, designed by world-renowned architect John Portman (see ch. 51 & 63). You can dine on the 70th floor with 360-degree vistas of the city. To the right, the building topped off with a block pyramid is one of the newer downtown skyscrapers, Suntrust Plaza (transitioning to Truist), which opened in 1992 in the northern part of Downtown. Our skyline changes frequently, becoming a whole new backdrop.

When the CDC (see ch. 20) published its blog post, *Preparedness 101: Zombie Apocalypse*, in almost the time it takes a bitten person to transform into a zombie, that post became the most visited page on the CDC's website… ever! Take care when taking photos here. You're on a bridge, and the skyline can be mesmerizing. Don't get hit and turn into a zombie yourself!

Address Jackson Street NE (where it crosses over Freedom Parkway), Atlanta, GA 30312 |
Getting there Bus 899 to Parkway Drive and Highland Avenue or to Jackson Street and
Highland Avenue | Hours Unrestricted | Tip Krog Street Tunnel is one of the best spots
for street art, a popular destination for photographers and tourists alike (1 Krog Street NE,
www.atlanta.net/things-to-do/krog-street-tunnel).

49 Japanese Lantern
A 325-year-old gift from our sister state

Before the Atlanta Botanical Garden was formed, there was a Japanese Garden in what was then part of Piedmont Park. It had been created in the 1960s by the Atlanta Bonsai Society and contained mostly the miniature trees. It was almost lost forever because of bonsai thieves.

In 1963, while it was flourishing, Minaminippon Broadcasting Co. in Kagoshima Prefecture, Japan, gifted us with an ancient Japanese lantern. Three years later, in 1966, Georgia Governor Carl Sanders helped establish a sister state/prefecture relationship between Georgia and Kagoshima. Fukuoka, of the Kyushu region in Japan, became Atlanta's sister city in February 2005. In 2020, the gifted lantern, today positioned at the Japanese Garden's west entrance, will be approximately 325 years old.

The Japanese Garden was resurrected, completed on May 9, 1980. In 1981, the Japan-America Society and the Atlanta Botanical Garden hosted a formal tea event when the Japanese Garden was officially dedicated. With the objective of creating a space of serenity, Japanese gardens are generally monochromatic, save for a few pops of color in the spring from azaleas and irises, and in autumn from the brightly-colored Japanese maple leaves. The focal point in this garden is a large Virginia pine, shaped to look like a bonsai.

Among the Japanese plantings are Japanese maples, dwarf conifers, and a weeping Japanese persimmon tree. The bamboo planted here in the early 1980s was brought over directly from Japan. There's a *machia*, or covered waiting bench that is traditional in tea ceremonies. There's also a *chōzubachi,* a stone basin used as a purification ritual before a tea ceremony takes place. A moon gate was added in 1983. The plantings on the Japanese Garden's pathways are from other parts of Asia, outside of Japan. Today, the Atlanta Bonsai Society hosts their popular annual Bonsai Show at the Garden.

Address 1345 Piedmont Avenue NE, Atlanta, GA 30309, +1 (404) 876-5859, www.atlantabg.org, info@atlantabg.org | Getting there Bus 27 to Piedmont Avenue at The Prado | Hours See website for schedule | Tip One hour north of Atlanta is Gibbs Gardens, which boasts 220 acres of display gardens, including a large Japanese garden with 2,000 Japanese maples of 100 varieties (1987 Gibbs Drive, Ball Ground, www.gibbsgardens.com).

50__Junkman's Daughter
Delight in shopping for the obscure and alternative

When you spot the giant flying saucer protruding from the building over the front door, you'll know you're in the right place. Yes, you're in for an out-of-this-world shopping experience at Junkman's Daughter. A few of the items you'll find here include clothing, costumes, wigs, jewelry, accessories, toys, gifts, candy, posters, games, figurines, plants, books, cards, a fully stocked tobacco shop, local artists' works, and almost every Halloween costume you could possibly want. And then there are the shoes! Climb up the red, 20-foot, high-heeled shoe to browse and try on some of the most eclectic shoes you've ever seen. Treat your feet to white patent-leather platform disco shoes, spiked biker boots, or sequined stiletto booties.

Pam Majors, actually the daughter of a junkman, started in 1982 what would become Junkman's Daughter, "Atlanta's Alternative Super Store." She initially stocked it with items from her parents' home and some of her intuitively brilliant selections. Sadly, Pam passed away in 2016, but her son, Moss Mills, now owns this unique, shiny jewel of a store. Originally located around the corner on Euclid Avenue, and then the corner of Euclid Avenue and Colquitt Avenue NE, Junkman's Daughter moved to its current location on Moreland Avenue, growing the business from 1,000 to 10,000 square feet!

If you've been here before, this is not the Junkman's Daughter of the 1980s or 1990s. Since Moss took the reins, armed with an education in business, plus retail and wholesale experience, the store transitioned from a merchandise shock-value focus to an obscure, can't-find-anywhere-else, and fashion-forward approach to stocking its shelves. That's not to say that they're no longer edgy, because they totally are. If you're ready for a super fun, off-the-charts shopping experience, this is a destination you want on your must-visit list.

Address 464 Moreland Avenue NE, Atlanta, GA 30307, +1 (404) 577-3188, www.thejunkmansdaughter.com | Getting there Bus 6 or 102 to Moreland Avenue and Euclid Avenue | Hours Mon–Fri 11am–7pm, Sat 11am–8pm, Sun noon–7pm | Tip For some of the best Mexican food in all of Atlanta, head down Euclid Avenue to El Bandido Mex Mex Grill. Try the ceviche or a burrito bowl, both delicious and Instagramable! (1083 Euclid Avenue NE, www.elbandidomexmexgrill.com).

51 Les Lions d'Atlanta

Bet you don't know their names

If you ask an Atlantan about *The Lion of Atlanta*, many will tell you that it's the larger-than-life, white Georgia marble, 1892 sculpture in Oakland Cemetery marking the gravesites of thousands of unknown Confederate soldiers who perished in the Atlanta Campaign of 1864. They'd be right, of course, but there are other lions in the city, including the real and magnificent lions at Zoo Atlanta.

But there are four others downtown that are sculptural perfection. Perhaps one of the reasons that even many locals don't know their names is that they have the same name as the lion in Oakland Cemetery, except plural, and in French: *Les Lions d'Atlanta*.

Many Atlanta residents know of the great John Portman (see ch. 48 & 63) as the late 20th-century architect of our city and the mastermind behind many of our downtown buildings, including the Westin Peachtree Plaza, the Hyatt Regency Hotel, and the Marriott Marquis, which had the world's tallest atrium when it opened in 1985. John Portman commissioned Olivier Strebelle, a globally renowned Belgian artist, to create the two pairs of guardians of the Marriott Marquis Hotel, where they have stood watch since 1986. *Les Lions d'Atlanta* (The Lions of Atlanta) are modern, monumental bronze figures of lions beloved by residents. John Portman designed, created, or is otherwise responsible for quite a few beautiful works of art in the Downtown area.

In a pop-culture moment, prior to a multi-million-dollar hotel renovation completed in 2016, Dragon Con conventioneers had started cosplaying the Marquis' carpet. As camouflage, cosplayers could lay on the floor and disappear into it – steampunk costumes were made with the pattern, Storm Troopers painted with the pattern, parade trucks were covered with the pattern, and even R2-D2 wore a tie with the carpet pattern. Years after being replaced, Marquis carpet pattern costumes continue making appearances at Dragon Con.

Address 265 Peachtree Center Avenue NE, Atlanta, GA 30303, www.marriott.com/
hotels/travel/atlmq-atlanta-marriott-marquis | Getting there Bus 816 to Peachtree Center
Avenue and Baker Street | Hours Unrestricted | Tip Head to the Buckhead for another
magnificent, awe-inspiring animal sculpture, *The Great Fish* or *The Giant Fish* that has stood
over the Atlanta Fish Market since 1995. The copper statue has been called the largest fish
sculpture in the world and the restaurant has a stellar reputation (265 Pharr Road NE,
www.buckheadrestaurants.com/restaurant/atlanta-fish-market).

52 Lifting the Veil of Ignorance

The legacy of Booker T. Washington

Booker T. Washington (1856–1915) was an American educator, author, and orator. At the main entrance of Booker T. Washington High School is an exact replica of Booker T. Washington tribute, *Lifting the Veil of Ignorance*, a bronze sculpture by Charles Keck. An inscription reads: *He lifted the veil of ignorance from his people and pointed the way to progress through education and industry.* The original sculpture can be found at Tuskegee University, a historically Black college in Tuskegee, Alabama, where Washington was the first president and first teacher.

Washington was born into slavery and rose to become one of the most revered Black intellectuals of the 19th century, founding the National Negro Business League, an initiative supported by Andrew Carnegie. His infamous conflicts with Black leaders like W. E. B. Du Bois over segregation certainly caused a stir, but today, he is remembered as one of the most influential speakers of his time. In 1895, at the Cotton States and International Exposition, Washington gave a speech, known as the "Atlanta Compromise," to a mixed, albeit segregated, audience, which brought him to the national forefront. He called for Black progress through education and entrepreneurship, rather than directly challenging the disenfranchisement of Black voters.

A historical marker in Piedmont Park, near the 14th Street entrance, marks the spot where he gave his famous speech. He worked to provide education for Black Americans at a time when resources and support were not easily accessible. Booker T. Washington High School's mission is straightforward: "With a caring culture of trust and collaboration, every student will graduate ready for college and career."

Martin Luther King, Jr. graduated from the school in 1944 and entered Morehouse College at 15.

Address 45 Whitehouse Drive SW, Atlanta, GA 30314, +1 (404) 802-4600, www.atlantapublicschools.us/btw | Getting there Blue or Green Line to Ashby | Hours Unrestricted from the outside only | Tip In 1973, Atlanta elected its first African-American mayor, Maynard Jackson. At the age of 35 he was the youngest Atlanta mayor elected and would serve three terms. His final resting place in Historic Oakland Cemetery is marked by a monument turned diagonally so that he can keep watch over his beloved city for eternity (248 Oakland Avenue SE, www.oaklandcemetery.com).

53__ The Living Building
A regenerative building gives more than it takes

The Kendeda Building for Innovative Sustainable Design has perhaps the highest "cool factor" of any other building in Atlanta. Open, operating, and offering tours today, their goal is for it to achieve Living Building Challenge (LBC) 3.1 certification, the world's most rigorous sustainable design and performance standard for buildings. The certification criteria encourage buildings that are regenerative, meaning that they give back more than they take from the environment. Project teams must meet all imperatives and provide actual performance data from at least 12 months of continuous occupancy and operations to prove it. They're working diligently to achieve Living Building certification in 2021. The Kendeda Building is, for the moment, a one-of-kind building for the Southeast.

Shan Arora, director of the Kendeda Building, speaking to what's most unique about the structure, said "My background is public policy, so for me, the best aspect of the building is that it removes the 'it can't be done here' argument. Yes, we can create a building in the Southeast that is regenerative!" The multilevel building has stunning salvaged wood that dominates its interior spaces. There's a rooftop for studying, relaxing, and even beekeeping. Georgia Tech occupied the building in September 2019, and its primary use is education of students in classrooms and class labs. Subjects taught here include chemistry, geology, biology, and physics.

They've had a share of fun in creating this architectural and environmental masterpiece. There's a huge animated mural on the lower level highlighting the building's sustainable water systems. And who is this "Kendeda," you ask? The Kendeda Fund gives $50 to $60 million annually in grants focused around social equity and the natural environment. Kendeda is derived from the names of the three children of Kendeda Fund founder Diana Blank.

Address 422 Ferst Drive NW, Atlanta, GA 30313, +1 (404) 385-4142, www.livingbuilding.gatech.edu | Getting there Bus 14 to 10th Street NW at Greenfield Street NW | Hours Unrestricted from the outside, tours available Fri 2pm | Tip At the intersection of science, art, and technology on Georgia Tech's campus is a 3,000-pound sculpture by Robert Berks of renowned physicist and Nobel laureate Albert Einstein (349 Ferst Drive NW).

54 Loew's Grand Bricks

A Gone With the Wind *treasure hidden in plain sight*

Houston's Restaurant on Peachtree Road may be part of a chain, but it's unique in one key way. Look for the small brass plaque that notes that an interior wall was built using bricks from the Loew's Grand Theatre, where the movie *Gone With the Wind* premiered in 1939.

Laurent DeGive, a Belgian consul, purchased an unfinished building at the corner of Marietta and Forsyth Streets downtown, and he transformed it into an opera house in 1870. DeGive's Opera House was later occupied by the Columbia Theater, and then by the Bijou Theater. The building was demolished in 1921. In December of 1926, a subsidiary of Loew's, Inc. leased the entire property for a term of 60 years. The property was renamed Loew's Grand, home of Metro-Goldwyn-Mayer (MGM) films. According to the *Atlanta Constitution* on March 5, 1978, the Loew's "…reached its zenith of glory with a presentation of the world premiere of Margaret Mitchell's 'Gone With the Wind.'" Other premieres here included, *Singin' in the Rain*, *Ben-Hur*, and *Doctor Zhivago*.

In January 1978, a fire destroyed most of the top three floors of the Loew's Grand. The theater had closed in June 1977, and there were efforts underway to restore and preserve the theater for its historic significance. The fire, which some believed to be arson, torched those dreams. Atlanta was feeling deflated with the loss of the Loew's Grand, coming on the heels of other losses, such as the Carnegie Library (see ch. 19), the Forsyth Building (see ch. 44), and an 1885 fire station at Five Points.

But some artifacts from the Loew's Grand survived. There is a section at the rear of the balcony of the Fox Theatre with chairs from the Loew's Grand, and the Road to Tara Museum in Jonesboro has chairs and a brass movie poster frame, in excellent condition. The Georgia-Pacific Tower now stands where the Loew's Grand had entertained so many Atlantans.

Address 2166 Peachtree Road NW, Atlanta, GA 30309, +1 (404) 351-2442, www.houstons.com/locations/atlanta-peachtree | **Getting there** Bus 110 to Peachtree Road NW and Colonial Homes Drive N | **Hours** Daily 11:30am–10pm | **Tip** The Apollo 6 Command Module is on display at the Fernbank Science Center. It was the last unmanned flight of Project Apollo (156 Heaton Park Drive, www.fernbank.edu).

55 Madame

She's still an "outrageous old broad"

Born in Dawson, Georgia, Wayland Parrott Flowers, Jr. would go on to make puppetry history with "Madame," who now resides at the Center for Puppetry Arts, along with countless other puppet celebrities. Madame, clad in gorgeous gowns and "summer diamonds" ("Some are diamonds, some are not."), came to life in the mid-1960s and would perform with Flowers for more than two decades, garnering television spots and shows during the 1970s and 1980s, including a long run, replacing Paul Lynd in the Center Square, on the game show *Hollywood Squares*. She was a regular on *Laugh-In* and *Solid Gold*, and she was the star of her own syndicated sitcom in 1982, *Madame's Place*. Flowers was a pioneer as one of the first mainstream entertainers who was openly gay.

You'll find puppets from nearly every culture on the planet here at the Center for Puppetry Arts, which is home to the Worlds of Puppetry Museum. The museum has almost 5,000 artifacts in its permanent collection. Its three main galleries are the Jim Henson Gallery, which houses the single largest collection of Jim Henson puppets and artifacts in the world; the Global Gallery, where you'll find Madame herself; and the Dean DuBose Smith Special Exhibits Gallery. There are also two theaters that produce more than 600 performances each season. You can also enjoy more than 50 unique educational offerings. There's also some programming just for adults, which are not nearly as racy as some of Madame's shows in Las Vegas, but kids are not allowed.

Wayland Flowers passed away at 48 years old in October 1988, but his name lives on – kind of. He was the inspiration behind the first name of Waylon Smithers, a fictional character on *The Simpsons*. The 1974 hand-and-rod puppet of Madame was gifted to the Center for Puppetry Arts by Marlena Shell, Flowers' last manager, to whom he had bequeathed his estate.

Address 1404 Spring Street NW, Atlanta, GA 30309, +1 (404) 873-3391, www.puppet.org,
info@puppet.org | Getting there Gold or Red Line to Arts Center | Hours Tue–Fri
9am–5pm, Sat 10am–5pm, Sun noon–5pm | Tip Bring the kids to Legoland Discovery
Center, one of only a handful in the United States, where you can build, play, ride, race, learn,
see – and eat too (3500 Peachtree Road NE, www.atlanta.legolanddiscoverycenter.com).

56 Margaret Mitchell's Scandalous Dance

Blackballed by the Atlanta Junior League

Margaret Munnerlyn ("Peggy") Mitchell's face was splashed all over *The Atlanta Journal* after dancing the "French Apache" (pronounced *ah-PAHSH*) at her debutante ball in 1921 at The Georgian Terrace. The dance, popular in Parisian nightclubs, was more than risqué. It demonstrated abuse – real grabbing and simulated slapping – and then Mitchell added a passionate kiss that got her blackballed by the Junior League of Atlanta. Many years later, the Junior League would invite Mitchell to their *Gone With the Wind* premiere party. She declined.

Mitchell assumed numerous personas over her far-too-brief life, and The Georgian Terrace played host to some of them. In 1935, Harold S. Latham, an editor for Macmillan Publishers, visited Atlanta in search of Southern literary talent. A friend of Mitchell's told Latham that she had written a book, which Mitchell had kept almost entirely secret. Latham approached her about it, and she insisted that it wasn't ready. So Latham gave up, and Mitchell's friend quipped to her that she was far too serious to be an author. Angered by their chiding, she gathered chapters she had already written and took them to Latham's hotel, The Georgian Terrace, where she handed over the manuscript at their lobby meeting. Today, the space that was the lobby is now the glamorous Livingston Restaurant + Bar.

In December 1939, the Atlanta premiere of *Gone With the Wind* was at the Loew's Grand Theatre, razed in the 1970s. During the several days of movie-related events, Vivien Leigh and her husband Laurence Olivier, and Clark Gable and his wife Carole Lombard, stayed at The Georgian Terrace. Mitchell would join them for the festivities. Following a private conversation with her, Clark told reporters that she was one of the most fascinating women he'd ever met.

Address 659 Peachtree Street NE, Atlanta, GA 30308, +1 (404) 897-1991, www.thegeorgianterrace.com | **Getting there** Red or Gold Line to North Avenue | **Hours** Unrestricted, see website for hours | **Tip** You can visit Historic Oakland Cemetery to pay your respects to this Pulitzer Prize-winning author. Family members are buried on each side of Margaret Mitchell's tombstone – she's on the Marsh side, and her parents are on the Mitchell side (248 Oakland Avenue SE, www.oaklandcemetery.com).

57 Miss Mamie's Cupcakes
Two-time TV baking champion

Mild-mannered Mamie Doyle has a competitive side. Majoring in art in college, Mamie worked at a bakery in Mackinaw, Michigan and fell in love with the craft. But there was one career hurdle: she didn't know how to bake. She moved to Marietta, Georgia, staying with a cousin. "I come from a large family," she says. "I know all 68 of my cousins!"

She attended Le Cordon Bleu, the same culinary education institution that Julia Child attended in 1950, at their Tucker, Georgia campus. To graduate, she had to do a six-week externship. She found a cupcake bakery on Craigslist that the owners were looking to sell. Mamie's last day of her externship became her first day as the new owner of that shop, today's Miss Mamie's Cupcakes.

That was October 2009. Mamie's parents and brother helped renovate the shop then and keep it updated. In very short order, Mamie applied to compete on the Food Network's show, *Cupcake Wars*. Following an extensive application process and a grueling, 16-hour day of filming and competing, Mamie emerged victorious! It would be six months before the episode aired (March 25, 2012), but as soon as it did, business tripled. But she didn't stop there. She was approached by Cooking Channel's *Cake Hunters* and won that competition too with an eight-tier wedding cake that was feminine for the bride and chocolate-Guinness cake layers for the groom – and it had a secret compartment with a stash of beer!

The shop is lovely. It's directly off Historic Marietta Square and features delightful window displays that have won multiple holiday window display competitions. One side of the shop features cases of cupcakes, cakes, cookies, and cheesecakes – clearly moving beyond a cupcake shop to a full-fledged bakery. The other side has a comfortable seating area, where you can enjoy the best tasting cupcakes in Metro Atlanta. Try Mamie's favorite, the Coconut Lemon.

Address 156 Roswell Street SE, Marietta, GA 30060, +1 (678) 290-9811, www.missmamie.com | Getting there Gold Line to Arts Center, then bus 10 to Marietta, and then CobbLinc bus 15 to Roswell Street at Waddell Street | Hours Tue–Sat 11am–7pm | Tip Here on the weekend? Come early to the year-round Marietta Farmers Market, where you'll find around 65 vendors on Saturdays (year-round) and about 25 on Sundays (May–October). It's pet-friendly, too (65 Church Street, Marietta, www.mariettasquarefarmersmarket.com).

58 MLK's Nobel Peace Prize
A dinner that would change Atlanta forever

The leader of the American Civil Rights Movement, Dr. Martin Luther King, Jr., was born and raised in Atlanta. The youngest person to ever receive a Nobel Peace Prize at the time, at only 35 years old, King was honored for his nonviolent resistance to racial prejudice in the US. You can see his 23-carat gold medal on display at the Martin Luther King, Jr. National Historic Park, near his birth home.

King's return to Atlanta was met with mixed reactions. Were it not for Atlanta's Jewish community, particularly Rabbi Jacob M. Rothschild, the racial prejudice still rampant in 1965 Atlanta may not have granted Dr. King a celebratory gala following his being awarded the Nobel Peace Prize, at least not a celebration that included *all* of Atlanta. Rothschild, along with Catholic Archbishop Paul Hallinan, Morehouse College President Benjamin E. Mays, Atlanta Constitution Editor Ralph McGill, and Mayor Ivan Allen formed a core group of organizers who were determined to host a significant banquet in downtown Atlanta at the Dinkler Plaza Hotel (razed in 1972).

Others supported the gala as well, including J. Paul Austin, president, chairman, and CEO of Coca-Cola from 1962–1981, and proponent of civil rights, who actually threatened to relocate the company were King not appropriately celebrated. Austin told Atlanta's top business leaders, "It is embarrassing for Coca-Cola to be located in a city that refuses to honor its Nobel Prize winner. We are an international business. The Coca-Cola Co. does not need Atlanta. You all need to decide whether Atlanta needs the Coca-Cola Co."

Rabbi Rothschild and colleagues drew 1,400 guests to the gala. It was the South's first public racially integrated banquet. Martin Luther King, Jr. gifted those 1,400 guests, on Wednesday, January 27, 1965, a magnificent 20-page speech. The original manuscript can be found at the Atlanta History Center.

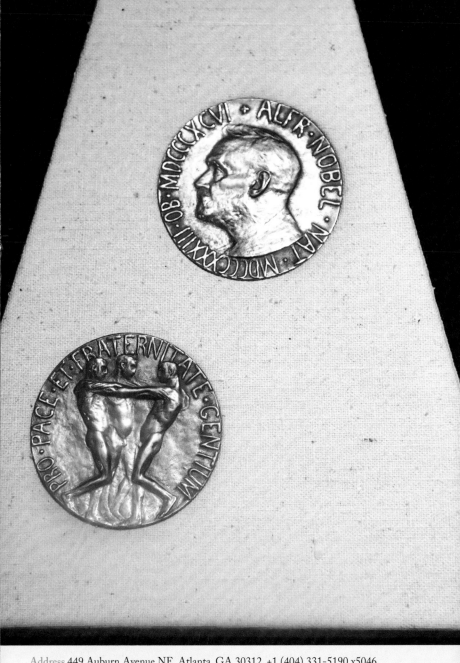

Address 449 Auburn Avenue NE, Atlanta, GA 30312, +1 (404) 331-5190 x5046,
www.nps.gov/malu/index.htm | Getting there Bus 3 or 899 to Jackson Street NE at
Old Wheat Street NE | Hours Daily 9am–5pm | Tip See Georgia's only other Nobel
Peace Prize, awarded to President Jimmy Carter, at the Jimmy Carter Library & Museum
(441 Freedom Parkway NE, www.jimmycarterlibrary.gov).

59 MLK Statue

A beacon for civil and human rights

Facing Liberty Plaza, Martin Luther King, Jr. Drive, and The King Center on a 3-foot-high Georgia granite platform stands a magnificent, 8-foot-tall statue of Civil Rights leader Martin Luther King, Jr. The original sculptor chosen to create the statue was killed in a motorcycle accident.

After that incident, the Georgia Council for the Arts invited artists to apply, and the pool was narrowed to four finalists. Local sculptor Martin Dawe of Cherrylion Studios received the commission. The front of the base features the large gold letters *MLK*, and the top of the base is engraved, also in gold letters, *I have a dream, that one day this nation will rise up and live out the true meaning of its creed: '...that all men are created equal!'*

Dawe's design for the sculpture comes from two major events and includes some nuances. The body of the sculpture was inspired by a photo of Dr. King when he was walking out of Alabama's Montgomery County Courthouse during the Montgomery Bus Boycott in 1956, sans his fedora. Dawe used Dr. King's face from photos of his "I Have a Dream" speech at the 1963 March on Washington, his most famous speech and a turning point in the Civil Rights Movement. As for the nuances, Dawe sculpted Dr. King stepping forward, signifying a new beginning, and sculpted his eyes looking a little to the left, so people will wonder what he could be thinking.

The sculpture was unveiled in a ceremony on the 54th anniversary of Dr. King's "I Have a Dream" speech. August 28 in Atlanta is usually sweltering, but that day it was 85°F and lightly overcast with a gentle breeze. It was perfect. What wasn't perfect was the tension in the air. Just weeks before, there were multiple deaths at a rally to prevent Confederate monuments from being taken down or moved. Dr. King stands today as a reminder to continue the "fight" for civil and human rights through peaceful protest.

Address Martin Luther King, Jr. Drive at Capitol Avenue, Atlanta, GA 30334 | **Getting there** Blue Line to Georgia State | **Hours** Unrestricted | **Tip** Tour the civil rights leader's birth home at the Martin Luther King, Jr. National Historic Park, a five-minute drive from the Georgia State Capitol. Tours are hosted by the National Park Service on Saturdays 10am–4pm, but get your free ticket the day you plan to tour at the Park's Visitor Center (www.nps.gov/malu/planyourvisit/birth-home.htm).

MLK

60 The Monetary Museum
The buck stops here, literally

Of the 12 Federal Reserve Banks in the United States, only a handful have museums, no two the same. The Atlanta Fed's Monetary Museum is a truly unique experience. You'll get to see part of the operation that shreds millions of dollars… every day! You also get to learn monetary policy and money handling, see rare coins and currency from around the world, and enjoy several interactive stations, too. The Story of Money exhibit chronicles the history of money, from the days of bartering to almost present day, including some early history of the Federal Reserve System, founded in 1913.

Opened in 2001, the formidable, 746,000-square-foot building resting on eight acres of prime real estate in Midtown was finished with White Cherokee marble from the same quarry in Tate, Georgia that supplied the marble for the Atlanta Fed's 1964 building in downtown Atlanta, as well as other public buildings in Atlanta and Washington, DC. Three of the eight acres are landscaped green spaces and public plazas, all great places to rest, people-watch, or enjoy a lunch from one of the many nearby eateries. Five marble columns from the Atlanta Fed's original 1918 building line the front public plaza facing bustling Peachtree Street. On the column closest to the main entrance is a 3,300-pound, 16-foot-wide cast bronze eagle originally from the Bank's 1964 building.

An especially fascinating exhibit in the "Cash Corridor" room is a display of large denomination notes, including $100 bills and the rarely-if-ever-seen-in-real-life $100,000 Gold Certificate. Would you rather have a bill with President McKinley's depiction or one with the engraved likeness of Salmon Chase, who wasn't a president? Believe me, you want to go with Chase. He was a chief justice and secretary of the treasury, and you'd have $10,000 in your pocket, although the McKinley $500 note is nothing to scoff at. But even the coins in your pocket have a fascinating history.

FEDERAL RESERVE BANK OF ATLANTA

Address 1000 Peachtree Street NE, Atlanta, GA 30309, +1 (404) 498-8500, www.frbatlanta.org/about/tours/museum.aspx | Getting there Red or Gold Line to Midtown | Hours Mon–Fri 9am–4pm | Tip All that money put you in the mood to splurge? Head to Phipps Plaza in North Buckhead, where you'll find Tiffany & Co., Dolce & Gabbana, Prada, Gucci, Versace, and a plush movie theater with a bar (3500 Peachtree Road NE, www.simon.com/mall/phipps-plaza).

61 Mummies at the Carlos

Meet the oldest mummy in the western hemisphere

The placard above the linen-wrapped figure in the Michael C. Carlos Museum simply reads *Mummy*. The oldest mummy in the western hemisphere was from Egypt's Old Kingdom, Dynasty 6, 2345–2181 B.C., and acquired in 1921. His head, hands, and feet were reattached to the body. This mummy, displayed laying on its side as was customary in burials from the period, is wrapped in tree resin-soaked linen. This early style of mummification was more concerned with the shape of the deceased's body over the body's preservation.

The Ancient Egyptian collection dates to 1876, when a museum was created on Emory University's first campus in Oxford, Georgia. The artifacts were moved to Emory's main campus in 1919. The museum's current location is named for philanthropist Michael C. Carlos, who funded the museum's design and subsequent redesign. The entrance is a pyramid-shaped portal, which is both appropriate and enticing. The Carlos Museum made national headlines following a 10-mummy purchase from a museum in Niagara Falls, New York. Clues and thorough examination led Emory teams to believe that one of the mummies was Ramesses I, grandfather of Ramesses the Great. After a celebrated exhibition at the museum, the mummy was gifted back to the people of Egypt as a goodwill gesture on behalf of the citizens of Atlanta.

Beyond the vast Egyptian collection, including numerous mummies and and sarcophagi, including that of Iawttayesheret, you'll find art and artifacts from Nubia and the Near East. There's another gallery featuring objects and life-size statuary from Greece and Rome. The Americas Gallery features maps inlaid on the floors to show you what part of the continent the artifacts you're viewing are from. Modest in size but plentiful on splendor are collections from Africa and Asia, as well as a gallery featuring a collection of works on paper from the Renaissance to the present.

Address 571 South Kilgo Circle, Atlanta, GA 30322, +1 (404) 727-4282, www.carlos.emory.edu | **Getting there** Bus 6 or 36 to North Decatur Road NE at South Oxford Road NE | **Hours** Tue–Fri 10am–4pm, Sat 10am–5pm, Sun noon–5pm | **Tip** Tour the 1929 Fox Theatre and see the Egyptian Ballroom, which features a relief of Ramses II. This pharaoh built more monuments and sired more children than any other Egyptian king (660 Peachtree Street NE, www.foxtheatre.org).

62 My Parents' Basement
Your new favorite comic book bar

Imagine having a dream about owning a comic book store… with a bar… and that dream coming true! True story: it did in 2012 when friends Lawson Wright, Tim Ensor, and Dave DeFeo came into a cache of more than 25,000 comic books – in a friend's parents' basement! This treasure trove led to pop-up shops, eBay sales, and "comic book yard sales," where they'd sell comic books 50 pounds at a time. By 2015, they'd raised enough capital to make their dream of opening a comic book bar come true. And they named it, aptly, My Parents' Basement.

A rare combination, this comic book store with a bar is actually so much more. There's the full-service bar, a full-service restaurant with a large patio, a comic book store offering primarily new comics – New Comic Book Day on Wednesdays are especially busy – and comic book "starter kits," boxes of 100 comics of a specific character or comic universe, as well as graphic novels, and other books. There's a modest but fun toy section. They have a killer arcade with 10 state-of-the-art pinball machines, including Guardians of the Galaxy, Deadpool, Jurassic Park, and Star Wars. There are some emulators too, so you can play classic video games, but on new machines.

The store, bar, and restaurant are decorated with hundreds of personal collections and fan-contributed comic book action figures, reaching all the way to the ceiling. The genre-specific vignettes (*Star Wars*, *The Muppets*, etc.) are great fun too. There are many works of art, some fan-contributed, some for sale. Their bestsellers are single-issue comic books, Three Tavern's "A Night on Ponce" IPA, and cheeseburgers. The menu features traditional pub fare, but as a sweet surprise, about one-third of their menu is vegetarian/vegan. In the warmer months, they harvest from an on-site garden. The bar features 32 taps, part of 100+ taps within a one-mile area – customers love their craft beer!

Address 22 North Avondale Road, Avondale Estates, GA 30002, +1 (404) 292-4607, mpbcbcb@gmail.com | Getting there Blue Line to Avondale | Hours Sun–Thu 11am–11pm, Fri & Sat 11am–midnight | Tip Three Taverns Craft Brewery, among those featured at My Parents' Basement, is less than a mile away. Visit their Parlour for "Belgian-inspired, American-styled craft beers" (121 New Street, Decatur, www.threetavernsbrewery.com).

63__Naked Ballerinas

Calm down – it's art on Peachtree Street

Conceived and designed by globally renowned architect and developer John C. Portman, Jr., *Ballet Olympia* is a pair of larger-than-life bronze female nudes with ribbons waving around them. This work is inspired by and adapted from an original 34-inch sculpture by Paul Manship (1885–1960). Portman's dancing females are 15 feet high and mounted on separate 8-foot-tall bases. They're Portman's tribute to Manship, the sculptor who created Rockefeller Center's *Prometheus*.

The headline on the front page of *The Atlanta Constitution* on Thursday, December 17, 1992, a week after the unveiling, read, "Nude statues turning heads." The article includes quotes from citizens that ranged from "Demeaning!" to "Lovely." They were quite the controversy for some, but that was nearly 30 years ago. Today, they're part of the tapestry of beloved Atlanta public art.

Manship's sculpture was titled *Maenad* (1953). A maenad is a female disciple of Dionysus, Greek god of fertility and wine and later considered a patron of the arts. The maenad would travel, collecting tribute to Dionysus. If nothing was given, the maenad would create chaos, according to waymarking.com, in the form of "uncontrolled sexual behavior, ecstatic frenzy, wild dancing, intoxication, etc." John Portman (see ch. 48 & 51) supported the arts. He was a collector, and he too was an accomplished painter and sculptor – you can see some of his other works nearby. Early on in his career, he pioneered the role of architect-as-developer, which allowed him greater opportunities to incorporate his design concepts.

Regardless of where one's level of appreciation for *Ballet Olympia* lands, the dancers certainly make for a striking entrance into Downtown. Atlanta and the world lost Portman on December 29, 2017 at the age of 93. His legacy lives on in remarkable art and architecture in Singapore, Beijing, Shanghai, Brussels, and coast-to-coast in the United States.

Address 303 Peachtree Street, Atlanta, GA 30308 | Getting there Gold Line to
Peachtree Center | Hours Unrestricted | Tip Five professional dancers split from the Atlanta
Ballet to create the magnificent Terminus Modern Ballet Theatre, which often performs at
the Westside Cultural Arts Center and in Serenbe, a community in Palmetto, Georgia
(760 10th Street NW, www.terminus-serenbe.com).

64 National Pencil Company

Lynching inspires two very different organizations

The National Pencil Company (NPC) went bankrupt, and the original downtown building on Forsyth Street was razed long ago. But this was the site of the horrific murder of 13-year-old Mary Phagan on Saturday, April 26, 1913 that would lead to the lynching of factory superintendent Leo M. Frank. When the jury declared him guilty two years later, there were cheers heard throughout the neighborhood. Frank was Jewish, and it seemed that the response was fueled by anti-Semitic propaganda during the two years after the murder, including songs sung near the courthouse by Fiddlin' John Carson (see ch. 38).

Two years after Frank's conviction, Georgia Governor John Marshall "Jack" Slaton commuted the sentence from death to life imprisonment due to doubts about the verdict. Soon after, a group of 25 men, including several prominent leaders, removed Frank from a state prison and drove more than 100 miles to a field in Marietta, Georgia that faced Mary Phagan's childhood home. Knowing death was near, Frank removed his wedding ring and asked that it be delivered to his wife. It was.

Isolationist Thomas E. Watson, twice a presidential candidate, wrote editorials said to have influenced Frank's conviction and lynching and that fueled the rebirth of the Ku Klux Klan by renewing racism, anti-Semitism, and hostility toward Catholics, immigrants, homosexuals, and others. At the other end of the spectrum, the Anti-Defamation League (ADL) was founded in 1913, its mission: "Stop the defamation of the Jewish people and secure justice and fair treatment to all."

Frank was posthumously pardoned on March 11, 1986 at ADL's urging, as new evidence emerged over time. Today, the former NPC lot is a federal building. But you can still visit the very spot where both Mary Phagan and Leo Frank had both simply gone to work just hours before they would each meet their violent fates.

Address 37–41 South Forsyth Street, Atlanta, GA 30303 | Getting there Blue, Gold, Green, or Red Line to Five Points | Hours Unrestricted | Tip Leo Frank's final resting place is in New York and Mary Phagan is buried in Marietta City Cemetery, northwest of Atlanta (395 Powder Springs Street, Marietta, www.mariettaga.gov/242/Marietta-City-Cemetery).

65 Noguchi Playscapes

Playtime courtesy of world-renowned sculptor

Save for a few young families that live near the gate to Piedmont Park at 12th Street and Piedmont Avenue, most Atlantans are unaware of the significance of the Noguchi Playscapes, designed by world-renowned sculptor Isamu Noguchi (1904–1988). Noguchi was honored with the Kyoto Prize in 1986, a prestigious award to recognize those who have contributed significantly towards the betterment of humankind. He was also awarded the National Medal of Arts by President Ronald Reagan in 1987, the highest award given to artists by the US government.

Excited, energetic children enjoy this one-of-a-kind playground nearly year-round, flying on its swing sets, bouncing on its seesaws, climbing on sculpture after sculpture, but the piece that immediately grabs everyone's attention is the sky-blue slide that wraps around a giant white cylinder.

One of the 20th century's most important and critically acclaimed sculptors, Isamu Noguchi was born in Los Angeles, lived in Japan until age 13, and eventually moved to New York. Noguchi's first major commission was in the late 1930s. Completed in 1940, *News*, the plaque on the former Associated Press building, is one of the largest art deco works of art in Rockefeller Plaza in New York City. It was the only time that Noguchi worked in stainless steel. Troubled by the Japanese attack on Pearl Harbor, Noguchi became a political activist, founding an organization in 1942 dedicated to raising awareness of the patriotism of Japanese-Americans. Later, he voluntarily asked to be placed in an internment camp. His postwar art reflects his experience there.

There's a 47"-wide model of the Noguchi Playscapes in the collections at The Noguchi Museum in New York. Today the playscape continues to delight children and inspire contemporary designers to consider play as a strategy for building community and stimulating creativity in the everyday.

Address Piedmont Avenue NE at 12th Street NE, Atlanta, GA 30309, www.piedmontpark.org/things-to-do/playgrounds | Getting there Gold or Red Line to Midtown | Hours Daily 6am–11pm | Tip If the kids aren't exhausted, take them to the Children's Museum of Atlanta adjacent to Centennial Olympic Park (275 Centennial Olympic Park Drive NW, www.childrensmuseumatlanta.org).

"When an artist stops being a child, he stops being an artist"
-Isamu Noguchi

PLAYSCAPES
Rededication: September 9, 1996

On the 20th Anniversary of its creation, Isamu Noguchi's "Playscapes" was restored thanks to the generous contributions of

KAJIMA CONSTRUCTION SERVICES, INC

with the support of the

PIEDMONT PARK CONSERVANCY
HIGH MUSEUM OF ART
ISAMU NOGUCHI FOUNDATION, INC.
&
CITY OF ATLANTA

Kajima gratefully recognizes the volunteer efforts of its subcontractors and suppliers who assisted in the restoration of this world-renowned work of art:

Andrew Electric Company, Inc.
Benise Dowling & Associates, Inc.
Construction Materials Ltd., Inc.
Duron Paints and Wallcovering
Henley Painting and Wallcovering, Inc.
Hepaco, Inc.
Landers Landscape, Inc.

Metro Waterproofing, Inc.
Porter Steel, Inc.
Pride Roofing, Inc.
Pro-Tec Plumbing, Inc.
Tebarco Mechanical Corporation
United Tool Rental
West Georgia Electric

66 Old Car City USA
4,400 cars on 40 acres – a photographer's dream

Most transportation enthusiasts will love Old Car City USA, the world's largest classic car junkyard. It's a photographer's dream. You'll find 4,400 classic cars, most of them American-made, as well as trucks, buses, vans, SUVs, RVs, bicycles, and much more. While the predominant color here is rust, you'll be surprised at just how colorful a place this is. You can even paint a car yourself in The Car Art Circle.

Elvis Presley is in the house. In the gift shop is the last car that the King of Rock 'n' Roll ever purchased, just a couple of months before he passed away. He purchased the car in Los Angeles and drove it off the lot himself. He then headed over to the home of his hair stylist and presented the car as a gift.

Also within Old Car City's 40 acres are seven miles of hiking trails. The trails are kept clear, but everything else is left to nature. You'll get to the car that a journalist dubbed the "Two-Ton Flower Pot," a name that stuck and that has inspired numerous photographs and quite a lot of art by owner Dean Lewis. Mother Nature is strong in the junkyard too. A tree seedling emerged under the rusted-out floorboard and grew straight through the windshield. Another nearby car has a tree that grew out of its front grille, looking like the hungry car is eating the tree.

Old Car City started as a general store in 1931. Today, there's a restaurant there, and the "new" store is across the street. Lewis, whose parents started the original general store, was born in that general store. He has numerous vocations, and painting is a more recent venture – he has some fascinating pieces. Ask him about his works of art. But, long before painting, Dean created "Styrofoam cup art," most of the cups covered by pen. His collection is housed upstairs in what he calls "The Junkyard Galleery." He has used almost 4,000 Styrofoam cups as canvases, almost equal in number to his cars.

Address 3098 Highway 411 NE, White, GA 30184, +1 (770) 382-6141, www.oldcarcityusa.com | Getting there By car, drive north on I-75 to exit 293, right on Highway 411 | Hours Tue–Sat 9am–4pm | Tip On your way back to Atlanta, visit Tellus Science Museum in nearby Cartersville. Their Millar Science in Motion gallery features transportation vehicles from Kitty Hawk to the Moon. They have helicopters, trains, boats, rockets, spacecraft, and a 1903 electric car (100 Tellus Drive, Cartersville, www.tellusmuseum.org).

67__Old Fourth Distillery

Go pee inside the bookcase – it's allowed

In the style of a Prohibition speakeasy, the bathrooms at Old Fourth Distillery (O4D) in Old Fourth Ward, the first legal distillery in Atlanta since before Prohibition, are hiding in plain sight. Look for a bookcase filled with colorful and realistic volumes when you need to answer nature's call and step through for the facilities. There are indeed some books for sale here, but not in the bathroom.

The distillery's design is wholly purposeful, from the sleek and stylish bottle designs to their custom-fabricated copper CARL still, made by Germany's oldest distillery fabricator since 1869. Every bottle of O4D product is made by hand in their 1,100-square-foot distillery. Their systems run so efficiently that it takes only three people to create the fermentations, do the distillations, bottle, and package all of their products, which include vodka, gin, bourbon, and Lawn Dart, a limoncello-esque beverage they've billed as "just a little bit dangerous and a whole lot of fun!" Their Straight Bourbon Whiskey is Atlanta's first and only Bottled-in-Bond bourbon, meaning that it's "the product of one distillation by one distiller at one distillery," plus some other strict requirements that make it a wholly unique experience.

Go on one of their tours and learn about the distillation process, fermentation, and their hand-bottling process, and then enjoy a tasting. Check out O4D's Finely Crafted: Cocktails & Comedy events every other Wednesday in The Locker Club on Edgewood Avenue, their Prohibition-style cocktail lounge in their tasting room. While you're there, pick up a bottle or a few and treat yourself to a souvenir, too.

You can find Old Fourth Distillery libations all over Georgia – click the "Find It" tab on their website to locate a restaurant, store, or bar convenient to you. Just know that there's nothing like getting it from the source!

Address 487 Edgewood Avenue SE, Atlanta, GA 30312, +1 (844) 653-3687, www.o4d.com |
Getting there Bus 809 to Boulevard SE at Edgewood Avenue SE | Hours Mon – Sat
8am – 6pm, Sun 10am – 5pm | Tip Head to the Painted Pin, an upscale boutique bar, bowling,
and entertainment destination (737 Miami Circle NE, www.thepaintedpin.com).

68 __ Olympic Flame Lit by Ali

Kicking off the 1996 Olympics

On the morning of Tuesday, September 18, 1990, all of Atlanta waited with bated breath for the announcement from Tokyo of the next host of the Games of the XXVI Olympiad.

"*At-lan-taaaaaa!*" Celebrations ensued.

On Friday, July 19, 1996, nearly six years later, shrouded in more mystery than perhaps any Olympic torch lighting in modern history, gold-medal Olympian and world-renowned boxer Muhammad Ali emerged to ignite a ball of flame that flew into the air to ignite Atlanta's Olympic Cauldron, officially opening the 1996 Summer Olympic Games. In 2016, ESPN ranked that moment when Ali ignited the flame on the 100th anniversary of the modern Olympic Games as the 8th most memorable moment out of 100 sporting events in the past 25 years. The 1996 Olympics garnered an estimated 3.5 billion television viewers.

Former Atlanta mayor and UN Ambassador Andrew Young would call the iconic torch itself "an embarrassment" – an assessment that not all Atlantans agree with – and stated that he would have preferred it be designed by someone like architecture legend John Portman (see ch. 48 & 51). The Olympic Tower received a refurbishment in recent years, marking the 20th anniversary of the 1996 Summer Olympic Games, but these days it's illuminated on an erratic schedule. Today, the Olympic torch that he ignited opening the 1996 Summer Olympic Games has an uncertain future. Perhaps it will be dismantled, or perhaps it will be relocated to Centennial Olympic Park. Or perhaps it will be celebrated where it is, attracting tourists and locals to a neighborhood that is seeing a surge of growth and development since GSU has occupied the nearby former Olympic Stadium.

In the year when Atlanta won the bid for the centennial Olympic Games, Ali was inducted into the International Boxing Hall of Fame. In 2005, he was awarded the Presidential Medal of Freedom.

Address 513–637 Capitol Avenue SE, Atlanta, GA 30312 | Getting there Bus 42 to Hank Aaron Drive SE and Fulton Street SE | Hours Unrestricted | Tip Just south of the Olympic Cauldron you can take in a Georgia State Panthers football game in what was our Olympic Stadium, repurposed for the Atlanta Braves after the 1996 Games and more recently for Georgia State University (755 Hank Aaron Drive SE, www.stadium.gsu.edu).

69 The One Equestrian Statue

Famous for all the wrong reasons

Believed to be the only equestrian bronze statue in Atlanta proper is the monument of General John Brown Gordon, riding his horse and facing the intersection of Washington Street SW and Martin Luther King, Jr. Drive SE.

Gordon was unaccomplished in his early life. He attended the University of Georgia, but he mysteriously withdrew before graduation. With the outbreak of the US Civil War, Gordon was made a captain – without having had any military training. He excelled and became one of Robert E. Lee's most trusted three-star Confederate generals. Following the war, Gordon was a vigorous opponent of Reconstruction and is believed by many historians to have been the leader of the Ku Klux Klan in Georgia during the late 1860s. He served as a US Senator from 1873 to 1880, and again from 1891 to 1897. He also served as the 53rd governor of Georgia from 1886 to 1890. He died in 1904 in Miami and is buried in Historic Oakland Cemetery. The statue was erected three years later in 1907.

The 1877–1879 Constitutional Convention voted in 1877 to move the state capital to Atlanta permanently and, in 1879, accepted the city's offer of the five-acre City Hall/County Courthouse tract, which was conveyed to the state in 1880. In 1883, the legislature finally appropriated $1 million for the construction of the new capitol, specifying that only Georgian materials be used, unless the cost of local materials proved prohibitive. Governor Henry D. McDaniel directed much of this process and, along with Governor John B. Gordon, oversaw the Capitol Commission.

In stark contrast to the anti-Reconstructionist statue, also on the Capitol grounds that Gordon had a hand in constructing, are sculptures of two famous civil rights leaders, both Nobel Peace Prize Laureates, Martin Luther King, Jr. (see ch. 58) and Georgia Governor and US President James Earl "Jimmy" Carter (see ch. 76).

Address 206 Washington Street SW, Atlanta, GA 30334 | Getting there Blue or Green
Line to Georgia State | Hours Unrestricted | Tip Travel north on Interstate-85 to the
Medieval Times Atlanta Castle and revel in chivalry, bravery, and equine beauty and grace
from times long ago (5900 Sugarloaf Parkway NW, www.medievaltimes.com/plan-your-
trip/atlanta-ga).

70 __ Out Front Theatre

Atlanta's only LGBTQIA+ theater

Out Front Theatre Company's first production in October 2016 was *Priscilla, Queen of the Desert: The Musical* with full-on glitter, glam, and a giant high-heel shoe! It was their introduction to the world as Atlanta's only 100% LGBTQIA+ professional theater, which happens to be 500 miles from any other professional theater with the same mission – "to tell LGBTQIA+ stories." When you attend a performance here, you'll see tasteful telltale signs that you've arrived somewhere "different" and it's fabulous. There's a full bar, there may be disco balls here and there, and the lobby is also "The Concourse of Community," adorned with full-size flags that represent "…the diversity and vibrancy of every individual that comes into this space." There's a poster near the front door that tells what each of the current 23 flags represent, ranging from Gay Pride to Transgender Pride to Straight Ally.

Out Front's season is October through May, offering five shows per season. Throughout the year they open their doors to other organizations, further strengthening the local LGBTQIA+ community. In addition to its five shows per season, Out Front Theatre is available for for rentals, offers education programming, and hosts special events. They've hosted Out on Film, Atlanta's LGBTQ film festival; Voices of Note, Atlanta's gay men's chorus and women's chorus; and many others.

The plays and musicals produced at Out Front are those that are important to, enjoyed by the LGBTQIA+ community at large, or are written by playwrights from within the community. Out Front Theatre was bravely launched – business license, 501(c)(3) status, and its inaugural season announced – before they had a space in which to perform them. Producing artistic director and founder, Paul Conroy, landed in the West Midtown neighborhood, one of Atlanta's hottest spots for dining, shopping, and entertainment.

Address 999 Brady Avenue NW, Atlanta, GA 30318, +1 (404) 448-2755, www.outfronttheatre.com | **Getting there** Bus 12 to 10th Street and Brady Avenue | **Hours** Check website for show times | **Tip** 7 Stages Theatre in Little Five Points offers a wide range of programming for a wide range of audiences, focusing on the social, political, and spiritual values of contemporary culture, with a primary emphasis on international work (1105 Euclid Avenue NE, www.7stages.org).

71 Paralympic Legacy Monument

Honoring the triumph of the human spirit

Nestled in a manicured landscape, the Paralympic Legacy Monument in Centennial Olympic Park bears the names of over 3,000 athletes who participated in the 1996 Atlanta Paralympic Games. The people whose names are engraved in gold won a medal. A spiral sculpture holds a large medallion inscribed, *The Triumph of the Human Spirit*. And there's a list of athletes' achievements at the games. The Paralympic torch to light the cauldron and officially open the games was itself lit from the eternal flame that burns at the tomb of Dr. Martin Luther King, Jr. It was carried by 1,000 people.

"To be surrounded by people who believe in you is one of life's most precious gifts," said Christopher Reeve, the master of ceremonies, to a crowd of 64,000 attendees at the Opening Ceremonies of the 1996 Paralympic Games. "Look around you and see how many people believe in you." It was only 15 months earlier that Reeve, known around the world for this portrayal as DC Comics' Superman on the big screen, was thrown from a horse and suffered a spinal injury that left him a quadriplegic for the rest of his life. Coincidentally, 1996 was also the first year that a para-equestrian dressage competition at the Paralympic Games was held, featuring 61 riders from 16 countries.

The first Paralympic Games were hosted in Rome, Italy in 1960. Their predecessor, the Stoke Mandeville Games, were first organized in 1948. Since 1976, the Paralympic Games have mostly been hosted in the same city as the Olympic Games. In 1996, 3,310 athletes from 103 countries competed, participating in 19 sports. During nine days of competition in Atlanta, 269 new Paralympic records were achieved. On the same side of the park, along Centennial Olympic Park Drive NW, are numerous other plazas, sculptures, and features with quilt patterns, all honoring Olympic history in Atlanta.

Address NW corner of Centennial Olympic Park, corner of Baker Street NW and Centennial Olympic Park Drive NW, Atlanta, GA 30313, www.gwcca.org/centennial-olympic-park | **Getting there** Red Line to Peachtree Center; Atlanta Streetcar to Centennial Olympic Park | **Hours** Daily 7am–11pm | **Tip** Make a photo next to or "inside" the Olympic Rings! At the park entrance at Centennial Olympic Park Drive NW and Andrew Young International Boulevard NW there's a large, colorful sculpture of the Olympic Rings (www.gwcca.org/centennial-olympic-park).

72 The Peace Tree
A world away from war

On Sunday, April 17, 1988, five acres of the Atlanta History Center's gardens were designated a Garden of Peace, the first in a global network of gardens dedicated to promoting peace. *The Peace Tree* is a 14-foot bronze sculpture by an artist from the Republic of Georgia, Georgi "Gia" Japaridze. It was part of an art exchange with the city of Tbilisi, Georgia, Atlanta's sister city in the Caucasus, west of the Caspian Sea. The sculpture was dedicated on Sunday, September 24, 1989, with the mayor of Tbilisi in attendance.

The centerpiece sculpture is five life-size figures holding hands around a 14-foot tree with doves in its branches. The Atlanta sculpture in the Atlanta–Tbilisi exchange was created by Sergio Dolfi, originally from Italy and a resident of Atlanta since 1973. His sculpture *Birds*, cast in bronze from an original carving in Australian wood, was installed in the second Garden for Peace in Tbilisi, also in 1989.

Gardens of Peace, today, is a network of approximately 20 gardens around the world, from Atlanta, Georgia to Tbilisi, Georgia; from Kenya to Korea; and from California to Hiroshima, Japan. The founder of The Gardens of Peace was Atlanta local Laura Dorsey Rains, who went to Japan during World War II when she learned that her husband had been wounded. A one-week visit turned into months. She comforted other wounded soldiers and listened to their stories. One day, seeking refuge from the horrors of war, she accidentally found a Japanese pocket garden, serene and a world away from the war. It was there that she had the idea for Gardens of Peace.

After the September 11 attacks in 2001, Atlantans visited the Garden of Peace at the Atlanta History Center and left flowers, candles, and notes. The attacks renewed interest in places of peace. Today, this Garden of Peace, the first of what is now many, continues to grow awareness of places of peace.

Address 130 West Paces Ferry Road NW, Atlanta, GA 30305, +1 (404) 814-4000, www.atlantahistorycenter.com, information@atlantahistorycenter.com | Getting there Red or Gold Line to Arts Center; bus 110 to Peachtree Road at East Paces Ferry Road NE | Hours Mon–Sat 10am–5:30pm, Sun noon–5:30pm | Tip Visit Olmsted Linear Park designed by Frederick Law Olmsted, the father of American landscape and the landscape architect for Central Park in New York City and the Biltmore Estate in Asheville, North Carolina (1788 Ponce de Leon Avenue NE, www.atlantaolmstedpark.org).

73 _ The Phoenix

Rising from the ashes like its hometown

As the mythical, fantastical phoenix rose from the ashes, Atlanta accomplished the same feat following Sherman's burning of the city during the American Civil War. Today, the phoenix is Atlanta's city symbol, even pictured on the official city seal, which bears the words, "1847 Resurgens, Atlanta, GA, 1865." Atlanta was founded in 1847 and rose from the ashes in 1865 after the war.

In 1967, on the occasion of Rich's department store's 100th anniversary, they announced to the public that, through its Rich Foundation, a statue would be gifted to the City of Atlanta. The store charged its design and display director, Dudley Pope, to design the statue. He, in turn, enlisted his assistant Jim Seigler for a conceptual idea. Sketches were sent to the foundation, where a committee picked the one that would be crafted. That sketch was delivered to Italian sculptor Gemba Quirino in the town of Pietrasanta, who created a miniature of the proposed sculpture. Atlanta Major Ivan Allen, Jr. approved.

Some locals complained because the sculptor was not an American, and others complained because the statue included a half-nude woman. Although Quirino is credited as the sculptor, he died unexpectedly in 1968. Feruccia Vezzoni was the actual sculptor of what stands in Woodruff Park today.

In preparation for the 1996 Olympics, the 22-foot-tall *Atlanta from the Ashes* sculpture was moved from its original location facing the nearby Georgia State Capitol Building to Woodruff Park, following a thorough refurbishment at City Hall East (today's Ponce City Market), and then rose once more on October 26, 1995.

The park holds public events that range from live jazz to movie screenings, from yoga to the annual German Bierfest. You can read a more detailed history of this sculpture and a comprehensive history of Rich's in *Rich's: A Southern Institution* by Jeff Clemmons.

Address 91 Peachtree Street NW, Atlanta, GA 30303, +1 (404) 546-6744, www.atlantadowntown.com/woodruff-park | Getting there Red or Gold Line to Peachtree Center; Atlanta Streetcar to Woodruff Park; bus 3, 40, 816 to Peachtree Street and Auburn Avenue NE | Hours Daily 6am–11pm | Tip At the other end of Woodruff Park, enjoy lunch or a moment of relaxation on a bench at the splendid curved wall fountain located at the northern tip of the park (91 Peachtree Street NW).

74__Pink House

Georgia treasures inside the Millennium Gate

Tens of thousands of people in cars pass the Millennium Gate Museum every day, most unaware of the treasures that await inside. Rodney Mims Cook, Jr., the mastermind behind the Gate Museum, was awarded the National Trust for Historic Preservation Prize in 1973 for his significant role in the Save the Fox campaign. He was only 14.

Today, Cook is at the helm of the National Monuments Foundation. He postulated that Atlanta should have a gate – after all, we're called the "Gate City." Originally a railroad town, the terminus of people traveling in every direction, we are the "gate" to the South. The name came from a desire to celebrate our achievements at the new millennium. Located in the relatively recent Atlantic Station, the Gate stands between the burgeoning Westside and Atlanta's cultural district.

While the Gate is an architectural marvel, and English Park where it resides is a delight, the multi-floor museum inside chronicles Georgia history from the Native American residents to the present day. There are three period rooms in the museum that capture Georgia's sense of "live, work, and play." Representing "play" is an exact replica of the 20th-century drawing room of Pink House, the Rhodes-Robinson home designed by Philip Shutze, architect of the Swan House, and Edward Vason Jones. In a *Marietta Daily Journal* article, Rodney Cook said that Lady Henrietta Spencer Churchill is "one of the greatest interior designers in the world" and that she was the curator for the three period rooms in the museum, noting that she found that Pink House has "the finest baroque salon in the western hemisphere."

To whet your appetite for exploration, also in this magnificent museum's collection is the 2nd-century *Bodmer-Hanna Papyri XIV* and *XV*, which contain the oldest written texts of the Lord's Prayer, purchased for the Vatican by Georgia native, Frank Hanna.

Address 395 17th Street NW, Atlanta, GA 30363, +1 (404) 881-0900,
www.thegatemuseum.org, info@thegatemuseum.org | Getting there Red Line to Arts
Center; bus 37 to 17th Street NW and State Street NW | Hours Mon – Sat 10am – 5pm |
Tip Placed on October 10, 1911 by older members of the Gate City Guard, the *Old
Guard Peace Monument* commemorates the Peace Mission of 1879 to promote peace and
the reunification of the country after the US Civil War (Piedmont Park at 14th Street,
www.oldguard-atlanta.org/peace-monument).

75_Plaza Theatre

Atlanta's longest running cast, performing Rocky Horror

While The Loew's Grand Theatre in downtown was running two screenings per day of *Gone With the Wind* in December 1939, the brand new Plaza Theatre, practically on the outskirts of town, hosted their gala opening with a screening of *The Women*, starring Norma Shearer and Joan Crawford, both Oscar-winning actresses.

The Plaza Theatre today is Atlanta's oldest operating and only independent cinema since 1939. And they're still setting records there. The original art deco marquee with blue chevrons and bright neon announces a midnight screening every Friday night – with a screen-accurate performance – of *The Rocky Horror Picture Show* by Lips Down on Dixie, which they've done every Friday night since December 2000. Talk about a time warp!

Lips Down on Dixie is Atlanta's longest running cast, and they're doing more than just having fun. Their Friday night shadow casting of *Rocky Horror* is purposefully put on to give young people, particularly those aged 17–29, a place to come and have fun and not be pressured to drink alcohol or consume illicit drugs that they might face in bars and clubs. They also keep things interesting by changing it up from time to time, making all the shadow cast characters superheroes, for example. You can also catch them headlining at the annual Dragon Con during Labor Day weekend.

There's a new ticket stand in the lobby, fashioned after some other art deco elements in the theater. The Legacy Lounge has art deco stenciled walls, art deco inspired pieces of furniture, and even the bathroom door handles are art deco. In the gallery is the concessions stand, featuring only classic theater treats and a new bar that offers in excess of 20 local craft beers and more. Plaza Theatre has a movie house organ and a dedicated organist, Ron Carter, who plays the instrument for a monthly silent movie and sometimes during the *Rocky Horror* pre-show.

Address 1049 Ponce de Leon Avenue NE, Atlanta, GA 30306, +1 (470) 410-1939, www.plazaatlanta.com | **Getting there** Bus 2, 102, or 816 to Ponce de Leon Avenue NE and North Highland Avenue NE | **Hours** See website for movie schedule | **Tip** SCADshow is a theater for Savannah College of Art & Design Atlanta's aTVfest and other SCAD events, and it also screens cinema blockbusters (173 14th Street, www.scadshow.com).

76 President Carter's Story

Peanut farmer, military, president, Nobel laureate

The Jimmy Carter Presidential Library and Museum invokes a sense of awe. You'll be mesmerized by the many accomplishments of this humble human being, who remains the only US president from the State of Georgia. You'll learn about Carter's hometown of Plains, and about the people who influenced his early life.

Carter was in the class of 1947 at the US Naval Academy, but he was enrolled in an accelerated program designed to get trained officers combat-ready during World War II. So he graduated early in 1946 as an ensign. He was an avid photographer during his Navy days – one of his cameras is on display. You can see an exact replica of the Oval Office as it was during the Carter administration. There are two doors, both on what would be the east side of the Oval Office. A small portion of that area is roped off, meaning that you can't roam the entirety of the space. But you can see the entirety of the room, including the president's Resolute Desk, with the American and Presidential flags behind it, and the Presidential Seal on the ceiling overhead. On loan from the US Navy, a model of the Revolutionary War privateer USS *Rattlesnake* sits on a table behind the desk. Even if you've visited the White House in Washington, this space is remarkable.

During Carter's years in the White House, Air Force One was warmly called "Peanut One." Coincidentally, Peanut One's pilot was also named Jimmy Carter. There's a gallery that showcases gifts from leaders around the world bestowed upon the president and First Lady Rosalynn Carter, a customary practice dating back many years. The range of gifts is profound and beautiful, representative of cultures the world over. The museum is massive, so schedule accordingly. Among the last items on your route are Carter's 2006 Grammy Award, Jimmy and Rosalynn's 1999 Medals of Freedom, and the president's 2002 Nobel Peace Prize.

Address 441 Freedom Parkway, Atlanta, GA 30307, +1 (404) 865-7100, www.jimmycarterlibrary.gov | Getting there Bus 816 to John Lewis Freedom Parkway NE and Ralph McGill Boulevard | Hours Mon–Sat 9am–4:45pm, Sun noon–4:45pm | Tip Take the self-guided tour of the Georgia Governor's Mansion, where future President Carter was only the second governor to live in the 30-room, Greek Revival mansion (391 West Paces Ferry Road NW, www.gov.georgia.govgovernors-mansion/tour-mansion).

77 __ Presidential Signatures

A surprising collection for a Western art museum

A Smithsonian affiliate museum, the Booth Western Art Museum has the largest permanent exhibition space for Western art in the United States at 120,000 square feet. It's also the largest Western-themed museum east of the Mississippi River and the second largest art museum in Georgia. And one of its greatest surprises is what it has beyond cowboy culture.

The museum's founders were also collectors of presidential and US Civil War materials. Believed to be a wholly unique collection, the Carolyn & James Millar Presidential Gallery houses a portrait and an original one-page, hand-signed document from each US president from George Washington to present day.

The founders of the Booth had been collecting presidential arti-facts since the 1970s. When the museum was founded in 2000, there were about 35 letters and a stellar collection of portrait photographs taken by the famed photographer Yousuf Karsh, stretching from Her-bert Hoover to G. H. W. Bush. These are presented in a dimly lit gallery to help keep them from deteriorating over time. In addition to the letters and portraits, there are several important sculptures depicting presidents including Thomas Jefferson, Teddy Roosevelt, and Jimmy Carter. The gallery is not named for the founders but in honor of Carolyn and Robert Millar, who were early patrons of the museum and mentors to the founders. They helped establish the endowment funds at both the Booth Western Art Museum and the nearby Tellus Science Museum.

There are a dozen galleries throughout the museum with content ranging from modern Western art, with a focus on living artists, to a spectacular sculpture gallery, where you'll find traditional and contemporary large-scale sculptures in a two-story atrium. A must-see is the 8 foot by 18 foot painting *Red Butte with Mountain Men*, painted in 1935 by Maynard Dixon.

Address 501 North Museum Drive, Cartersville, GA 30120, +1 (770) 387-1300, www.boothmuseum.org | Getting there By car, drive I-75 north to downtown Cartersville | Hours Tue & Wed, Fri & Sat 10am–5pm, Thu 10am–8pm, Sun 1–5pm | Tip Just around the corner, explore 200 years of Bartow County history from the Cherokee Indians to current day, all housed in the refurbished 1869 downtown courthouse (4 East Church Street, Cartersville, www.bartowhistorymuseum.org).

78__Rainbow Terrace

Where Henry Heinz was murdered

Nestled in the wooded suburb of Druid Hills is one of Atlanta's most beautiful homes, formerly known as Rainbow Terrace. It would keep that name until a burglar claimed the life of Henry Heinz in the late evening on September 29, 1943. Heinz was a noted banker, philanthropist, and husband to Lucy, the only daughter of Coca-Cola magnate Asa G. Candler.

The home had been burglarized numerous times during the previous three years. Likely skittish from past theft in 1928 of $120,000 worth of "traveling jewels" in Atlantic City, Heinz was determined to stop the burglaries. The night of his death, he struggled with the intruder. The burglar's thumb was shot, and then Heinz was shot four times, likely killing him instantly.

Lucy moved into a suite at the Biltmore Hotel (see ch. 17) and married Enrico Leide, the first conductor of the Atlanta Symphony Orchestra, on February 5, 1946, less than two years later, which contributed to suspicions that perhaps she was involved in her first husband's murder.

The origins of Druid Hills began with Joel Hurt who, in 1890, persuaded Frederick Law Olmsted, Sr., landscape architect of America's largest home, the Biltmore Estate, in Asheville, to visit some land Hurt had purchased. Olmsted agreed to prepare a plan for a new neighborhood. His preliminary plan was submitted in 1893, which included a linear park, today comprised of several small parks collectively called Olmsted Linear Park. Olmsted's firm presented a final plan in 1905, and his sons remained involved with the project until 1908. The Olmsted Brothers would later develop a plan for Piedmont Park. Not realized immediately, the area ultimately honors the brothers' 1912 plan.

Rainbow Terrace was divided into six condominiums in the original mansion, with 40 townhomes on the gated grounds. Today, the private residences are collectively called The Lullwater Estate.

Address 1610 Ponce de Leon Avenue NE, Atlanta, GA 30307 | Getting there Bus 2 to Ponce de Leon Avenue and Fairview Road NE or Lullwater Road NE | Hours Unrestricted from the outside only | Tip The home used in filming Oscar-winning film *Driving Miss Daisy* is literally around the corner and viewable from the outside only (822 Lullwater Road NE).

79 Randolph-Lucas House

Built for Thomas Jefferson's great, great-grandson

Arguments that Atlanta is in danger of tearing down everything that makes it unique are seemingly eons old. Case in point: the Randolph-Lucas House was once considered the last of its kind on Atlanta's most famous street, Peachtree. The 1924 Georgian-style house was built, moved, and moved again. It was first moved from its original location to just a few feet toward Peachtree to make room for a 10-story European Regency-style condominium building, constructed in 2000 in the heart of Buckhead at Lindbergh Drive NE. The house finally found its forever home on another of Atlanta's Peachtrees: Peachtree Circle in Ansley Park.

Atlanta architect P. Thornton Marye (see ch. 40), who also helped build the Fox Theatre, designed the grand home for Hollins Nicholas Randolph, whose great, great-grandfather was Thomas Jefferson, author of the Declaration of Independence and third president of the United States. Designed to look like Randolph's childhood home in Charlottesville, Virginia, it was later sold to Arthur Lucas, who owned a number of local theaters, and his wife Margaret, who lived there until she died in 1987. The house was used for special events for a short while and then sat vacant and approaching ruin. In Anne Rivers Siddons' 1989 novel *Peachtree Road*, she predicted that the Randolph-Lucas House would fall into disrepair and eventually be lost to history.

Fortunately, local preservationists would create a different storyline for the home. NewTown Partners, an Atlanta-based economic development consulting firm specializing in historic preservation, moved the home to 78 Peachtree Circle, then an empty lot in Ansley Park, where it became the private home of company founders Christopher Jones and Roger Smith. Sadly, Christopher passed away in January 2019 from complications from cancer, but not before securing the future of their beloved Randolph-Lucas House.

Address 78 Peachtree Circle NE, Atlanta, GA 30309 | Getting there Red Line to Arts Center; bus 37 or 110 to Peachtree Street NE and 16th Street NE | Hours Viewable from the outside only | Tip Among other P. Thornton Marye architectural projects is the 1906 St. Luke's Episcopal Church, which goes back to 1864 and was given cathedral status (435 Peachtree Street NE, www.stlukesatlanta.org).

80 Rare Amitabha Buddha
650-year-old Japanese Buddha at OUMA

A 650-year-old Buddha made its public debut in the US on Monday, September 15, 1986 in an exhibition titled, "The Many Faces of Buddha," at the Oglethorpe University Art Gallery, the predecessor to today's Oglethorpe University Museum of Art (OUMA). The Amitabha Buddha is seated in *vajrasana*, or lotus position, with both hands in the *dhyanasana mudra* gesture, meaning "contemplation." The 14th-century, 25-inch-tall Buddha is made from wood and *urushi*, or lacquer, with traces of gilding. Believed to have come from a temple near Oyama, Japan, the artifact was acquired by Gump's in San Francisco, probably in the early 1960s.

In 1962, Thomas Chandler, librarian at Oglethorpe University, entered into an agreement to acquire the Amitabha Buddha from Gump's on a payment plan of $80 per month. Two years before Chandler finished paying it off, the retailer shipped the Buddha to Atlanta. Lloyd Nick, an art professor at Oglethorpe University, gave up his professorship to become the first director of the new museum (OUMA) in 1992, as the museum absorbed many of the artifacts from the original art gallery. The Amitabha Buddha was among the first of the museum's acquisitions for its permanent collection. Not without coincidence, OUMA acquired the Buddha on a payment plan with Thomas Chandler, just as Chandler had done with Gump's decades before. Today, the museum's largest collections are 19th-century French paintings and Japanese art from the 14th to 20th century.

John Daniel Tilford joined OUMA in 2013. He was promoted to Curator of Collections in 2015 and tripled the museum's permanent collection within three years. "It's rare to have such an early work of Japanese art in this country, particularly for a university art museum," Tilford says of the Buddha. "People naturally gravitate toward its beauty, and that has set a standard for what's expected of our acquisitions."

Address 4484 Peachtree Road NE, Atlanta, GA 30319, +1 (404) 364-8555, www.museum.oglethorpe.edu | Getting there Gold Line to Brookhaven/Oglethorpe; bus 25 to Peachtree Road and Lanier Drive | Hours Tue–Sun noon–5pm | Tip Nakato Japanese Restaurant has delighted Atlantans and visitors alike since 1972. Be sure to visit their Japanese garden (1776 Cheshire Bridge Road NE, www.nakatorestaurant.com).

81 Ray Charles Sings...
"Georgia on My Mind" at the Capitol

Winner of 13 Grammy Awards, music legend Ray Charles performed "Georgia on My Mind" before a joint session at the Georgia State Capitol on Wednesday, March 7, 1979. Conceived and co-sponsored by John White, representative for Charles' birth city of Albany, Georgia, with representatives Peggy Childs, Cas Robinson, and William Randall, the idea of making Ray Charles' version of "Georgia on My Mind" the official state song became a reality. Following an overwhelming number of votes from the House and Senate, on Tuesday, April 24, 1979, the song was indeed designated Georgia's official state song.

"Georgia on My Mind" was first written and recorded by Hoagy Carmichael and Stuart Gorrell in 1930, coincidentally the same year that Ray Charles was born. Charles recorded the song 30 years later in 1960. It was the first of three number-one singles on *Billboard*'s "The Hot 100" list for the artist. In 2004, Jamie Foxx played Ray Charles in the blockbuster movie, *Ray*, which took home two Academy Awards and a Golden Globe.

Surprisingly, the Georgia Capitol Building is very open in both design and access, so much so that it's garnered the nickname "The People's House." The Capitol's north and south wings are available free of charge (catering and other services are available for a fee) for events, such as press conferences, meetings, speeches, or ceremonies. Visitors can go on a self-guided tour of the Capitol just by checking in with security at the Washington Street entrance. Be sure to tour the museum on the fourth floor (see ch. 100). People frequently ask if the gold on the Georgia State Capitol Dome is real gold. When the building went up in 1889, the dome was white. In 1958, Dahlonega, Georgia donated 40 ounces of gold to guild the dome, which was implemented immediately, and to let the world know that the first gold rush happened right here in Georgia.

Address 206 Washington Street SW, Atlanta, GA 30334, +1 (404) 463-4536, www.libs.uga.edu/
capitolmuseum, gacapitoltours@uga.edu | Getting there Blue or Green Line to Georgia State |
Hours Mon–Fri 8am–5pm | Tip Hear musicians from around the world at Rialto Center for
the Arts (80 Forsyth Street, www.rialto.gsu.edu).

82 Red Phone Booth

A speakeasy experience with Southern hospitality

Shhh… it's a secret! Yes, you do need to be a member or be acquainted with someone who knows the secret code to gain access to this remarkable speakeasy. The entrance is a red phone booth. Once inside the 1935 Kiosk No. 6, the iconic British red phone box, you'll pick up the receiver and then *dial* the code on the old school rotary phone. You'll be greeted by a speakeasy host, who will give you an introduction to the space and all of their offerings. Looking for the ultimate whiskey experience? Your search stops here. Red Phone Booth offers more than 180 whiskeys, with an extensive selection of rare libations. In alignment with the speakeasy experience, drinks have pseudonyms. Belly up to the "pharmacy" (bar) and order a "prescription" (cocktail), and enjoy the show! Perhaps an "ale-ment" (beer), or a "vaccine" (shot) or an "antioxidant" (wine) is just what the doctor ordered.

Red Phone Booth offers a glimpse into "civilized society" from January 17, 1920 to December 5, 1933, although these sorts of venues were not exactly legal at the time. Highly trained bartenders – perhaps the best in the city – arrive hours before opening time to prepare the bar, which features 100% fresh-squeezed juices including blood orange, mango, and cranberry, and double-reverse osmosis ice, hand chipped from 300-pound blocks. The area in the rear – the secret within the secret – is the Mafia Kitchen, complete with a pool table. This Prohibition-era experience features an exclusive "inhalant" program (cigars), with approximately 140 different cigars. Air turns over every four minutes, so even non-smokers can enjoy the atmosphere.

As with every aspect of the adventure here, this is a high-end, luxury experience set in a wholly relaxing atmosphere – there is a dress code (see website). Red Phone Booth is committed to giving their patrons an exceptional, upscale, and memorable experience.

Address 17 Andrew Young International Boulevard NE, Atlanta, GA 30303, www.redphonebooth.com, info@redphonebooth.com | **Getting there** Red or Gold Line or Atlanta Streetcar to Peachtree Center | **Hours** Mon–Fri 4pm–late, Sat 5pm–late, Sun 5pm–midnight | **Tip** The owners of Red Phone Booth also own Amalfi Pizza upstair the only eatery in Georgia to hold Associazione Verace Pizza Napoletana certification as makers of authentic, traditional *vera pizza Napoletana* (17 Andrew Young International Boulevard NE, www.amalfipizzaatl.com).

83_ Rhodes Hall
The Castle on Peachtree

Whether by design or pure luck, Rhodes Hall is one of the extremely few mansions remaining on Peachtree Street, where once the street was lined with them. The home was built by Amos Giles Rhodes, who arrived in Atlanta via his work on railroads. Soon after, he started a frame business. Because of the postwar levels of poverty, he designed a payment plan by mapping a collections route onto his sales route. And thus the modern pay-over-time arrangement was born. His frame business paved the way to the creation of one of the greatest furniture companies in the country. Rhodes was also a revered philanthropist.

The furnishings in Rhodes Hall are primarily the original fine European furniture that Mr. and Mrs. Rhodes preferred, ironically, and there are samples of the more commercial Rhodes Furniture on the second floor. The house was equipped with gas and electricity, rare at the time, as well as radiator heat, a call system, and an alarm system. Amos and his wife Amanda called Rhodes Hall "Le Rêve," or "The Dream."

She passed in 1927, and Amos followed the next year. He willed the Victorian Romanesque Revival home to their children, but by then they were grown and already established in their own homes. In 1929 the children deeded the home to the State of Georgia with the caveat that it could never be sold, never be torn down, and must be used for education and other purposes. Between 1930 and 1965, the home served as the State Archives, which Margaret Mitchell would use to conduct research, presumably for *Gone With the Wind*. Another Margaret Mitchell connection, the designer of this house created a duplicate of its hand-carved, mahogany staircase and put it in the home owned by Margaret's father on Peachtree Street just north of 17th Street, where she spent part of her youth. There's a historical marker where that home once stood.

Address 1516 Peachtree Street NW, Atlanta, GA 30309, +1 (404) 885-7800, www.rhodeshall.org | **Getting there** Red Line to Arts Center; bus 110 to Peachtree Street NE and Peachtree Circle NE | **Hours** See website for tour information | **Tip** There's another castle nearby, a historic home that has been numerous things over the years, including an art space and a restaurant. This wholly unique house was designed and built by Ferdinand McMillan as his retirement home, which he called Fort Peace. Today, it's called The Castle or Castle Atlanta (85 15th Street NE, www.facebook.com/castleatlanta).

84 Rodin's *The Shade*
The death and rebirth of the arts in Atlanta

Atlanta lost a vast majority of the city's most dedicated art supporters at 11:34am on Sunday, June 3, 1962. The Atlanta Art Association had been on a three-week tour of European art capitals, and on that day, their plane went down shortly after takeoff from Orly Field, near Paris. Of the 130 who perished in the crash, 106 were Atlantans, and so the city lost the core of her cultural and arts leaders, and 33 children and young adults lost lost one or both parents in the crash. Atlanta was devastated.

Following the crash at Orly Airport – at the time, the deadliest air disaster involving a single plane – sympathy from around the world came flooding into Atlanta, including $15 million to create a memorial building. The Memorial Arts Center was inaugurated on October 5, 1968. Renamed the Woodruff Arts Center in 1982, it is home to the High Museum of Art, Alliance Theatre, and the Atlanta Symphony Orchestra. The French government presented a gift of Rodin's *The Shade* to the city in memory of the Atlantans lost at Orly. The statue arrived in 1968. It was later moved to its current location on the High Museum of Art's lawn under an enormous ginkgo tree, and rededicated in May 1995. It's surrounded by a small wall engraved with the names of those lost in 1962.

The Shade was one of 186 figures in Auguste Rodin's *The Gates of Hell* sculpture depicting scenes from Dante's *Inferno*, a project that was to be a portal for Paris' planned Museum of Decorative Arts. Arguably the most recognized sculpture in the world, *The Thinker* was also part of that project. Our Rodin sculpture was cast from the artist's original mold in Paris.

Artist Andy Warhol, who has been exhibited and has permanent pieces displayed at the High Museum of Art, created a painting of the front page of the *New York Mirror* the day after the crash. *129 Die in Jet!* hangs in Museum Ludwig in Cologne, Germany.

Address 1280 Peachtree Street NE, Atlanta, GA 30309, +1 (404) 733-4200, www.woodruffcenter.org | Getting there Red or Gold Line to Arts Center | Hours Unrestricted | Tip Across the street at Colony Square is Alliance Française d'Atlanta, which offers classes, events, and more. They're in a joint facility with the German Cultural Center (1197 Peachtree Street, www.afatl.com).

85 Rogue Olympic Torch

One man's desire to leave an Olympic legacy

Perhaps the most frequently seen remnant of the 1996 Olympic Games hosted in Atlanta is Tazwell Leigh "Taz" Anderson Jr.'s *Centennial Tower*, which resembles an Olympic Torch. However, the golden flame in the cauldron was actually fashioned after the flame atop the Statue of Liberty's torch. Although not popular with the Atlanta Committee for the Olympic Games (ACOG), Anderson's "rogue" project came from a desire to leave a visual legacy that Atlanta had indeed hosted the Olympic Games.

Anderson was an athlete himself, having played football while attending the Georgia Institute of Technology (GaTech) and then played professionally for the National Football League (NFL), the St. Louis Cardinals and the Atlanta Falcons. After his football career, he became a real estate developer. One of his many projects, the 12-story steel tower directly across the interstate from the Olympic Village, has an observation deck 105 feet up, and there was an Olympic souvenir shop at the base. (Anderson was grateful that the ACOG didn't issue the building permits in Atlanta!) He charged $2 to climb the 123-foot tower, which many did during the Olympics and after. Centennial Tower has been closed for many years, but it continues to stand as an Olympic legacy, Anderson's original desire.

The official Olympic Cauldron (see ch. 68) and Olympic Rings stand today in Summerhill, near the former Olympic Stadium, now part of Georgia State University's sports programs. Anderson was inducted into the Georgia Tech Sports Hall of Fame in 1982 and also into the Georgia Sports Hall of Fame in 2006. He passed away in September 2016 at the age of 77. The following year, the Georgia Sports Hall of Fame, located in Macon, Georgia, created the Taz Anderson Service Award honoring "a Georgian who has distinguished him/herself through tireless and dedicated volunteer work in the realm of sports."

Address 70 3rd Street NW, Atlanta, GA 30308 | Getting there Gold Line to North Avenue | Hours Unrestricted from the outside only | Tip Taz Anderson also developed *The Peaches*, the two large peach sculptures near the north and south ends of "The Connector," where Interstate-85 and Interstate-75 merge as one.

86 Rufus M. Rose Mansion
A game of "What's Next?"

The dilapidated Rose Mansion, which holds promise for an exciting, although uncertain, future, was built in 1901 for Dr. Rufus M. Rose, founder of Four Roses bourbon. The home is one of only four urban mansions still standing that once proliferated Peachtree Street.

There is some speculation that Four Roses bourbon was given its name in 1906 when the four Rose family members were living in the Peachtree mansion. This state-of-the-art residence boasted gas and electricity, nine fireplaces, a ballroom on its third and top floor, and indoor plumbing! After the Roses passed away, the home went through many inhabitants, most often with boarders. Dr. Rose died on Monday, July 22, 1910. His body was laid in state in the library of the house. After a traditional funeral, Rose was afforded a Mason's highest honors. The front porch was removed in the 1930s.

Then, in 1945, James Elliot, Sr., purchased the house and opened J. H. Elliot's Antiques. His Atlanta Museum was housed on the second floor and was billed as "one of the South's oldest and most interesting museums," with over 2,500 "historical items," and artifacts that had belonged to Bobby Jones (see ch. 41), Margaret Mitchell (see ch. 56), and other prominent Atlantans. The museum showcased historical artifacts from Atlanta and around the world, including the first Japanese Zero fighter plane that had been captured by US troops in WWII, displayed in the small backyard.

The Atlanta Preservation Center used the Rose Mansion as its headquarters from 1999 to 2001 and then moved to their current headquarters in the L. P. Grant Mansion in Grant Park. Architect Emil Charles Seiz's design for the Rose Mansion was a simplified version of the aesthetic movement's Queen Anne-style architecture. Nobody knows what's next for this mansion, but many would like to see it restored to its former glory.

Address 537 Peachtree Street NE, Atlanta, GA 30308, www.atlantapreservationcenter.com/rose_on_peachtree | Getting there Bus 40 to Peachtree Street NE and Linden Avenue NE | Hours Unrestricted from the outside only | Tip The Rose Distillery is not in Atlanta, but head over to American Spirit Works (ASW) Distillery for a taste and a tour (199 Armour Drive, www.aswdistillery.com).

87 Samuel Spencer Bronze

First president of Southern Railway

Commissioned in 1909, a magnificent bronze statue of Samuel Spencer, president of six railroads and the first president of Southern Railway, has made multiple stops on its journey. After Spencer's untimely death, 30,000 Southern Railway employees paid for the statue, designed by sculptor Daniel Chester French and architect Henry Bacon. The pair collaborated on numerous projects, including the Dupont Circle Fountain and the Lincoln Memorial in Washington, DC. The Spencer sculpture may have been a prototype for the 19-foot, seated statue of Abraham Lincoln, which is made of Georgia white marble.

The Spencer bronze was officially dedicated on May 21, 1910, at Atlanta Terminal Station, where it stood for 60 years. When Terminal Station was razed, Spencer was moved to Peachtree Station in Brookwood (see ch. 40), Atlanta's only remaining passenger train depot. In preparation for the 1996 Olympic Games, under the Corporation for Olympic Development in Atlanta (CODA), the statue was relocated to Hardy Ivy Park (see ch. 36) and reunited with its base. Since 2009, the statue has graced the landscape of the Goode Building (Norfolk Southern offices) on Peachtree Street, its third Peachtree Street locale.

Spencer moved the company's services strategically away from dependence on agricultural transportation and focused on diversification and other initiatives. Southern continued to grow into a major US railway. Known as Norfolk Southern since 1982, today it's a Fortune 500 company.

Spencer was tragically killed at 6:10am on November 29, 1906, in a train collision in Virginia. It is believed that he and others died instantly while in their sleep. On the day of his funeral, all Southern Railway trains were briefly halted in his honor. *The New York Times* reported, "The South has lost one of the moving spirits in its recent revival, and America one of its leading railroad experts."

SPENCER
1906

Address 1200 Peachtree Street NE, Atlanta, GA 30309 | Getting there Red or Gold Line to Arts Center | Hours Unrestricted | Tip Today a special events venue, the Trolley Barn is an architectural gem designed in 1880. It was the hub for the first electric streetcar system in the United States (963 Edgewood Avenue, www.thetrolleybarn.com).

88 SCAD FASH

Fashion and film dressed to the nines

Perched on a hill overlooking the north end of the downtown Connector, the SCAD FASH Museum of Fashion + Film's building itself is a fashionista! The former credit bureau building today is a beacon for students studying fine arts – and serves as evidence that gray is indeed stylish and dynamic. When you arrive at the campus, follow the broad stripe that's the same color as the museum's logo. The line will deliver you to the entrance to the museum, several floors up. Watch for the clever signs announcing your progress on the way to your destination.

On the entry level, you'll pass by a beautifully appointed courtyard, also accessible from the museum lobby one level up, which is handsomely decorated. Within the museum are two exhibition galleries featuring designs by inspiring designers. In a recent exhibit of Guo Pei garments, you would have seen the spectacular yellow cape worn by Rihanna at the Met Gala. You can also see some of the museum's permanent collection online. Rarely on display, for example, is an original Mariano Fortuny "Delphos Gown" from 1907 and made of finely pleated black silk, cording, and glass beads. This gown was inspired by and named after the robes of the classical Greek bronze statue, *The Charioteer of Delphi* (470 B.C.), which was discovered in an archaeological excavation in 1896.

The museum employs student docents, who are trained tour guides. The museum also offers an audio tour that you can take using your smartphone or iPad. Comfortable and inviting, the SCAD FASH Film Salon shows SCAD-produced films. Previous visitors have enjoyed films on Oscar de la Renta, Carolina Hererra, Guo Pei, and Pierre Cardin. Perhaps your favorite designer is next. A must-not-miss destination, SCAD FASH Museum of Fashion + Film offers the school's students and faculty – and visitors, too – the wonderful opportunity to celebrate works of wearable art and remarkable filmmaking.

Address 1600 Peachtree Street NW, Atlanta, GA 30309, +1 (404) 253-3132, www.scadfash.org, scadfash@scad.edu | Getting there Red or Gold Line to Arts Center; bus 110 to Peachtree Street NE and Spring Street NW | Hours Tue & Wed, Fri & Sat 10am–5pm, Thu 10am–8pm, Sun noon–5pm | Tip If seeing such fine fashion has put you in the mood to shop, head to The Shops Buckhead Atlanta, where you'll find the likes of Hermes, Jimmy Choo, and Dior (3035 Peachtree Road NE, www.theshopsbuckheadatlanta.com).

89 Senoia Museum

From Princess Senoia to The Walking Dead

The town Senoia is about 40 minutes south of Atlanta, and it's the place to go on a zombie tour or dine at Nic & Norman's Restaurant, owned by Greg Nicotero and Norman Reedus of *The Walking Dead* fame. Or maybe you're at Senoia Raceway for car, kart, or motorcycle racing. But try stepping back in time to 1825, when Creek Indian Chief William McIntosh, also known as Tustunnuggee Hutke, negotiated and signed a treaty to cede a significant portion of remaining Creek lands to the US, thus breaking Creek Law. This crime led the Creek National Council to sentence a fellow tribesman to death for crimes against the Nation.

The town of Senoia is named after Chief McIntosh's mother Senoya, also spelled Senoia and Senoy. Locals pronounce the town "Senoy," and those visiting usually pronounce it with a "-ya" at the end.

The Senoia Historical Society Museum is housed in the Carmichael House, around the corner from downtown. The house was built by J. A. McKnight circa 1870, and he was the first resident in this historic home that now exhibits thousands of artifacts. The museum consists of five display rooms and a research library. Just inside the front door, visitors will see an antique telephone and photograph of McKnight, and the main hallway of the house serves as a photo gallery of contemporary events and portraits of Senoia citizens. Among the museum's artifacts are two 1827 land lottery deeds with leather state seals documenting the area's Native American presence and the lottery story itself. The exhibit rooms are organized chronologically.

Fast-forward a number of generations, and you'll learn about Senoia's role in film and television. There's a massive Riverwood Studios movie projector. *Fried Green Tomatoes* was in part filmed here, and more recently, much of season 2 through the series finale of *The Walking Dead* was filmed here – downtown Senoia is Woodbury in the series.

Address 6 Couch Street, Senoia, GA 30276, +1 (770) 400-3669, www.senoiaareahistoricalsociety.org | Getting there By car, I-85 South, south on Joel Cowman Parkway, right on Rockaway Road, right on Couch Street | Hours Fri & Sat 1–4pm | Tip Just around the corner on Main Street is Woodbury Shoppe, the official store for *The Walking Dead* merchandise and souvenirs. Be sure to go downstairs where you can see one of Daryl's motorcycles (48 Main Street, Senoia, www.woodburyshoppe.com).

90 Shutze's Porcelain

This noted architect was also a collector

Ask any local about famous Atlanta architects, and Philip Trammell Shutze's name will definitely come up. The Columbus, Georgia native is well-known as the architect of the 1928 Swan House at the Atlanta History Center, but he was much more than an architect. He was also a collector. A serious collector.

When you tour the Swan House, perhaps the most photographed structure in Atlanta, be sure to venture to the terrace level (some call it the basement), where you'll find a magnificent labyrinth of an exhibition, Mandarin Shutze: A Chinese Export Life, showcasing Shutze's love of porcelain. It will give you a glimpse into how he lived. You'll see table settings, covered dishes, tureens, sauce boats, platters, sweetmeat dishes, mustard pots, teapots, and so much more. An 18th-century fashion, some of the dishes you'll see are in the shape of animals or vegetables. Look for the extremely rare pair of delicate and intricate boar's head tureens from Qiánlóng, China, made in 1763.

Beyond his international travels, Shutze would use visits to historic sites as inspiration. Some of his favorite places were Colonial Williamsburg, the houses at Newport, and especially the Winterthur Museum in Delaware. In the exhibition you'll see architectural drawings of his Peachtree Street apartment. While living there, he amassed a collection that would fill wall and surface spaces – they were all covered in ceramics and works of art. He stored his Chinese porcelain in his oven, dishwasher, and guest bathroom.

If you were a guest in his home, you couldn't miss the fact that he was obsessed. But in the Swan House, you could easily pass the interior entrance to the terrace level, totally missing this magnificent collection. In one room of the exhibition, you'll see a portion of Shutze's apartment living room, with stunning furniture, art, china, porcelain, and even a section of his living room wall.

Address 130 West Paces Ferry Road NW, Atlanta, GA 30305, +1 (404) 814-4000, www.atlantahistorycenter.com | Getting there Bus 110 to Peachtree Road and East Paces Ferry Road NE | Hours See website for hours and tour information | Tip Shutze designed more than private homes. For another fine example of Shutze architecture, visit Glenn Memorial Church, built in 1931, on the Emory University campus (1660 North Decatur Road, www.glennumc.org).

91 Sister Louisa's

This CHURCH *is a bar – irreverent fun at its best*

In pristine white lettering covering the breadth and height of a blood red door, CHURCH-goers are warned: *Every time you exit here, Jesus kills a kitten.* Sister Louisa's CHURCH of the Livingroom & Ping Pong Emporium is the most irreverent fun you'll have in Atlanta. No, you don't have to be an irreverent person to "attend" this church, but you can't be too sensitive either. And visitors are fairly warned by bright neon signs on ground-floor windows conspicuously announcing, *CHURCH… it's a bar.*

As you walk up, a neon sign greets you with the distinctly Southern welcome, …*Come on in, Precious!* The walls at Sister Louisa's are completely covered with hundreds of pieces of "unique" religious art. Bar owner Henry Grant is also the artist who creates the works under the funky pseudonym "Sister Louisa." Reportedly, he opened the bar to have a place to showcase his art. The artworks adorning the walls – plus sometimes quirky furniture – of Sister Louisa's are all for sale, meaning that each visit could be wholly unique. True to its name, there is indeed a living room section upstairs here, as well as ping-pong tables, where they host tournaments on Monday nights. There is Church Organ Karaoke on Wednesday nights, with choir robes available should the spirit move you to don one while singing for Sister Louisa's parishioners. Hollywood celebrities have been known to get in on the fun.

Grant's signature artwork has "graced" the covers of books, including, *Bleachy-Haired Honky Bitch: Tales From A Bad Neighborhood* and *Confessions of a Recovering Slut: And Other Love Stories* by Hollis Gillespie. There's a confessional converted into a photo booth downstairs – but you might be wishing it was a confessional by the end of the evening. You're going to want to pull out your phone and snap some photos here – and immediately share them with your followers on Instagram.

Address 466 Edgewood Avenue SE, Atlanta, GA 30312, +1 (404) 522-8275, www.sisterlouisaschurch.com | Getting there Atlanta Streetcar to King Historic District | Hours Mon–Sat 5pm–3am, Sun 5pm–midnight | Tip When you've had enough ping-pong but want to keep playing games, head across the street to Joystick Gamebar for classic video arcade games, pinball, tabletop games, and "booze aplenty" (427 Edgewood Avenue SE, www.joystickgamebar.com).

92 Stargazing at GaTech
Stellar views from downtown Atlanta

There's only one telescope in downtown Atlanta strong enough to see the moon, planets, and stars, as well as power the Astronomy Department at the Georgia Institute of Technology, locally known as "Georgia Tech" or "GaTech." Southerners love college football – approaching the intensity of Europeans' love for soccer. So there are many who know and regularly attend Georgia Tech Yellow Jacket football games. In fact, one of its mascots was the subject of a *Jeopardy* question in 2018 (the answer: Ramblin' Wreck, a restored 1930 sport coupe that's been used at the school since 1961). But there's a hidden gem on campus.

It was a long and storied path for Dr. James "Jim" Sowell to get the 20-inch, Italian *Officina Stellare* telescope installed on the roof of the Howey Physics Building. But he succeeded, and today during Public Nights, young stargazers not only have access to Georgia Tech's Observatory, they're also learning about the solar system, stars, galaxies, and the universe, as well as astro-particle, electromagnetic, gravitational, and stellar astrophysics.

You'll be among some very smart people when you visit the observatory, as many of the department's students attend Public Night, too. But don't be intimidated because everyone here is friendly and welcoming. On any given visit, you might see the moon, or maybe Saturn and its rings.

Public Night is held once per month, usually on the Thursday closest to when the moon is at first quarter – a half moon. The orientation of the Sun, Earth, and Moon is such at these times that the shadows are evident, so it's easy to see the rugged surface of the moon and its craters and mountains. Public Nights are usually two to three hours but are dependent on rather clear skies. So watch for email and social media for announcements. These events are always free, but there's a fee to park at the Physics building.

Address 837 State Street, Atlanta, GA 30332, +1 (404) 385-1294, www.astronomy.gatech.edu | Getting there Red or Gold Line to Midtown | Hours See website for events. Dependent on the weather. | Tip After looking up, look down – into the water. Catch a swimming or diving competition at Georgia Tech's McAuley Aquatic Center, which was part of the 1996 Olympic Games (750 Ferst Drive, www.ramblinwreck.com/sports/c-swim).

93 Starlight Drive-In Theatre

Drive in, chow down, snuggle up

Starlight Drive-In Theatre is the last remaining drive-in theater in Atlanta and has been since the 1990s. It's one of only four operating drive-in theaters in all of Georgia. Swan Drive-In is located in Blue Ridge, Georgia, Tiger Drive-In is in Tiger, Georgia, and Jessup Drive-In is in Jessup, Georgia, near Savannah. Seeing a movie at Starlight Drive-In Theatre is now a wholly unique experience. You can see movies here every night of the week, current blockbusters in a range of genres. Unlike many small-town drive-ins, Starlight accepts credit cards and prices are reasonable especially compared to standalone or mall movie theaters.

The first domestic drive-in opened June 6, 1933, in Camden, New Jersey, the brainchild of Richard Hollingshead, son of the owner of a line of automotive products. He patented the idea and went on to achieve financial success. When the patent expired in 1949, other drive-in theaters popped up all over the country – including Starlight in 1949 – peaking in the 1960s with more than 5,000 drive-in theaters in the United States. Today, there are only a few hundred still in operation.

Starlight originally began as a single-screen theater before adding a second screen in 1956. It became a quad in 1981 and expanded to six screens in 1983. Today, your modest Starlight Drive-In movie ticket price often gets you a double feature. Be sure to visit the concession stand for your favorite movie treats, and Starlight also offers a selection of Mexican foods. Unlike the drive-ins of yesteryear, where you had to hang speakers on your window, today's movie sounds are broadcast through your car radio.

This theater redefines "double-feature" by also offering the public a weekend flea market! Market-goers will enjoy more than 300 vendors and full concessions. At this outdoor market you can find toys, clothes, crafts, antiques, and collectibles, and parking is free.

Address 2000 Moreland Avenue SE, Atlanta, GA 30316, +1 (404) 627-3641, www.starlightdrivein.com, info@starlightdrivein.com | Getting there For drive-in (you must be in a car), Interstate-20 East to Moreland Avenue, then south to the destination; for the flea market, bus 4 or 49 to Isa Drive SE at Moreland Avenue SE | Hours See website for movie times and flea market events | Tip Scott Antique Markets' tagline, "America's Favorite Treasure Hunts," is absolutely true. It's one of the country's largest flea markets, with more than 3,000 dealers coming in for four days every month (3650 & 3850 Jonesboro Road SE, www.scottantiquemarket.com).

94__The Superb

A presidential funeral procession on rails

Among the 90-plus items of rolling stock, including four working engines, that you can meander through at the Southeastern Railway Museum, just like rail passengers of yesteryear once did, is the only privately owned rail car to carry the body of a US president who died during his term. Warren G. Harding was a popular president until after his death, when scandals – sexual and financial – were revealed shortly thereafter.

The *Superb*, President Harding's private, heavyweight Pullman car, was donated to the museum in 1967. Harding traveled in this car on his "Voyage of Understanding," a two-month speaking and sightseeing tour to go out and connect with the American people in the West and gain support for his domestic and foreign policies.

Harding was the first US President to travel through Alaska. As a child, he had dreamed of becoming a locomotive engineer, and during that leg of his journey, his dream came true for 51 minutes in Alaska when he controlled the train. But then, the week before arriving in San Francisco, President Harding fell ill. He arrived in the city, where he passed away in his hotel room on Thursday, August 2, 1923, apparently of a heart attack. The following day, his casket was elevated inside the *Superb* so that mourners could pay their respects as the late president traveled from across the country and back to Washington, DC. Approximately 3,000,000 people lined the tracks as the train passed. The train arrived in Washington, DC's Union Station with the president's remains on August 7.

The museum offers an array of programming throughout the year, including caboose and engine rides, climb-on rides, an annual photography contest, and annual 5K, and much more. At the entrance of the museum is the relocated Duluth Depot, now a museum within itself featuring Native American history, railroad uniforms, and telegraph artifacts.

Address 3595 Buford Highway, Duluth, GA 30096, +1 (770) 476-2013, www.train-museum.org | Getting there Red Line to Doraville, then take Gwinnett County Transit bus 10B toward Sugarloaf to Gwinnett Transit in Doraville | Hours See website for seasonal hours | Tip See *The General*, one of the two engines from the Great Locomotive Chase, at the Southern Museum of Civil War and Locomotive History in Kennesaw, Georgia, approximately 30 minutes northwest of Atlanta (2829 Cherokee Street NW, Kennesaw, www.southernmuseum.org).

95 Sweet Auburn Curb Market

Miss D's and more

The Atlanta Municipal Market, founded in 1918, was established in response to a disaster in the city. Most know that Atlanta was burned toward the end of the US Civil War. But not as many people know that Atlanta burned again in the Great Atlanta Fire of 1917. By the time it was extinguished, the fire had claimed 200–300 acres and destroyed nearly 2,000 structures, leaving 10,000 people homeless – nearly five percent of the city's population. It was farmers who revitalized what was the epicenter of the city by gathering to sell livestock and produce. At first housed under a large tent, this open-air market was a huge success. The Atlanta Women's Club conducted a fundraising campaign to build a fireproof, brick structure which opened in May of 1924. Black people were not permitted to vend inside at that time but were relegated to sell their wares along the curb outside.

In the early 1940s, the market's basement served as a municipal air-raid shelter, as well as an emergency first-aid post. Also in the 1940s, the market flooded and cars outside were nearly submerged. In 1949, the city finally installed lighting along Auburn Avenue. History would see the area become home to many entertainment venues, churches, and Black-owned businesses, including one owned by Alonzo Herndon, who became Atlanta's first Black millionaire (see ch. 45). In fact, a 1956 *Fortune* magazine article described Auburn Avenue as "the richest Negro street in the world."

Today, the market boasts a number of present-day success stories. Dionne Gant moved here after Hurricane Katrina took nearly everything she owned. She started Miss D's Pralines, and people since have enjoyed her New Orleans sweets, popcorn, and candy apples. The market has also served as a business incubator. Grindhouse Killer Burgers started in the market and today boasts at least six locations.

Address 209 Edgewood Avenue SE, Atlanta, GA 30303, +1 (404) 659-1665, www.municipalmarketatl.com | **Getting there** Atlanta Streetcar to Sweet Auburn Market | **Hours** Mon–Sat 8am–6pm, Sun 10am–5pm; see website for individual merchant hours | **Tip** Hop on the Atlanta Streetcar from the market and visit a wide range of tourist attractions in the downtown and nearby areas, ranging from the King Center to Centennial Olympic Park to Oakland Cemetery (www.itsmarta.com/streetcar.aspx).

96__Terminus
Be afraid of more than zombies

[Spoiler Alert] When the residents of Terminus broadcast, "Sanctuary for all. Community for all. Those who arrive survive," they were, of course, lying. If you're a fan of AMC's hit series *The Walking Dead*, and you've seen Season 4 and 5, keep reading. Those who arrived at Terminus became fodder for the cannibals who lived there. But when not in the middle of the zombie apocalypse, the building that sat in as Terminus is a real former railroad terminus. The long, long lines of train cars you'll see sitting to the left of Terminus would be your first clue.

On the television show, under each of the top row of windows are large format letters spelling "TERMINUS." Terminus began as a sanctuary community, but horrors occurred, and that changed. Gareth (actor Andrew J. West), the leader of Terminus, captures Rick Grimes (actor Andrew Lincoln) and his group and keeps them in a rail car – once street side at the same location – preparing to have them for dinner – literally. We get to see just how badass Carol (actress Melissa McBride) is when she blows Terminus to smithereens!

In real life, the faded sign at the front gate reads *Atlanta Motor Shop*. The business behind the Terminus building and the property to the left of the entry road are both metalworks. If you drive here, be careful where you park. The streets are littered – not remnants of the zombie apocalypse, but reminiscent of it.

While you can't go up to or into the building, you have an excellent vantage point from atop a hill. There are fewer obstructions now than there were years ago, so you can see the whole façade you know so well from *The Walking Dead*. You don't need a zoom lens to get some decent photos of the building, but go ahead and bring it if you have one. One of the great things about this filming site is that it still looks as creepy as it did on television. Bring a friend when you come here - you don't want to face any hungry zombies by yourself.

Address 793 Windsor Street SW, Atlanta, GA 30315 | Getting there Bus 42 to Cooper Street SW and Hendrix Avenue SW | Hours Unrestricted from the outside only | Tip The building that served as the CDC in *The Walking Dead* is in fact the Cobb Energy Performing Arts Centre. The exterior somewhat resembles the Sydney Opera House, and the interior is reminiscent of The Kennedy Center (2800 Cobb Galleria Parkway, www.cobbenergycentre.com).

97 __ Theatrical Outfit
Atlanta's first desegregated restaurant

The mission of Theatrical Outfit, a professional theater in downtown Atlanta, is to "produce world-class theatre that starts the conversations that matter." Theatrical Outfit is repeating history. In 1962, in this very space, Herren's Restaurant, after a hundred hours of conversations with other restaurateurs, became the first restaurant in Atlanta to desegregate voluntarily – two years before the Civil Rights Act of 1964. Founded during the Great Depression, Herren's thrived in its Luckie Street locale in the 1940s–1950s in what was then called Restaurant Row. It was also the first restaurant in the city to have air conditioning. Herren's closed in November 1987, but history-making would continue in this space.

Theatrical Outfit was founded in 1976 and is Atlanta's second oldest-professional theater company. Looking for a permanent home in the early 2000s and having researched numerous locales, they kept coming back to the old Herren's. Thus Balzer Theatre at Herren's, home of Theatrical Outfit, opened in January 2005, when they launched the first of many seasons of plays and musicals. The first performance here was *Ain't Misbehavin'*, a musical revue tribute to the Black musicians of the Harlem Renaissance of the 1920s and 1930s.

In a city not known for art deco architecture, people often walk right past Theatrical Outfit because of the hustle and bustle on Luckie Street. So be sure to look up as you go in. At the top of the stairs on the second floor, there's usually a gallery of art or photography that relates to the current show on stage. So when you go for a break at intermission, take a little extra time and enjoy the displays that will enhance your theater experience. And look for the original Herren's sign in the stairwell! On the sidewalk out front, Theatrical Outfit has its own star-studded Walk of Fame, featuring the names of major donors.

Address 84 Luckie Street NW, Atlanta, GA 30303, +1 (678) 528-1500, www.theatricaloutfit.org, office@theatricaloutfit.org | Getting there Red or Gold Line to Peachtree Center; Atlanta Streetcar to Luckie at Cone | Hours See website for schedule and free tours | Tip Around the corner is the William Oliver Building, constructed in 1930 and Atlanta's first large building to be fashioned entirely in the art deco style, including a grand brass entrance. You can admire its art deco splendor from the sidewalk (32 Peachtree Street).

98__Tiny Doors ATL

An artist's huge contribution to Atlanta

Karen Anderson Singer grew up loving miniatures. She didn't play with dolls, but spent countless hours playing with dollhouses, often using clay to build tiny furniture and accessories for them. When this professional artist moved to Atlanta, she decided to launch a public art project and married her love of miniatures with her grand idea for Tiny Doors ATL. Today, you can find these 7"-high doorways throughout the city.

Karen's project does have some caveats. There are currently 18 doors in her numbered series, and they are not for sale – visiting them is always free, and she ensures each is wheelchair accessible. Most of the doors don't actually work, however, some of them do open, and some even feature augmented reality (AR). Using a device – phone, goggles, iPad, etc. – you can explore these AR-enabled doors to see objects around the door that aren't actually there. They're computer-generated scenes and objects that enhance the natural environment and tell a story, giving the viewer a wholly unique experience.

Karen constantly cares for and attends to maintenance issues on all of the doors. So each time you visit could quite possibly be a new experience. It's a good idea to visit the Tiny Doors ATL website before embarking on a tiny door adventure of your own. For example, *Door #1 Krog Street Tunnel* was installed in 2014 but was moved – still within Krog Street Tunnel – in 2017. And *Door #2*, also installed in 2014, just got a freshening up. Follow the evolution of your favorite doors via Instagram.

A delightfully unique way to explore Atlanta is by visiting all the Tiny Doors ATL installations throughout the city, a passion project by an artist and transplant from Michigan who wanted to gift something to her new hometown. Karen says, "It's not about doors. It's about community, interaction, and engagement. It's kind of a love note to Atlanta."

Address Various locations, www.tinydoorsatl.com, studio@tinydoorsatl.com | Getting there
Various locations | Hours Unrestricted | Tip When you visit *Door #1 Krog Street Tunnel*,
you're just a three-minute walk from Krog Street Market, a 1920s warehouse converted
into a gathering place with restaurants, eateries, sweets, and retailers (99 Krog Street,
www.krogstreetmarket.com).

99 __ Trilon Fountain

A refreshing visit with a German expressionist

Called "Georgia's German expressionist," Steffen Wolfgang George Thomas (1906–1990) was born in Fürth, Germany, but he lived the majority of his adult life in Atlanta, Georgia. Thomas was a multi-talented artist who also worked in the mediums of poetry, paint-ing, sculpture, metalwork, mosaic, watercolor, and others. The Trilon Fountain is a stationary copper sculpture of a cutout female figure with three flat sides, each one seeing through the other two. In the heart of Midtown, it's seen by millions every year, but few know its name or the artist's.

Thomas moved to the United States in 1930. In 1933 he met and dated local Atlantan Sara Douglass, an educator, and they were mar-ried only six weeks later. The *Atlanta Journal-Constitution* newspa-per captured them on their wedding day with the headline, "Steffan Thomas, Sculptor, Elopes with Atlanta Girl." Thomas became an American citizen in 1935. In 1941 they purchased a 50-acre farm in Stone Mountain, Georgia and built their home and an art studio…by hand. Thomas made his living through commissions and portraiture, but he decided to leave behind the rigors of clients who would not invite his particular artistic expression. He and Sara moved back to Atlanta in 1973 and had a Midtown art studio. The Trilon Fountain, made of copper, granite, and limestone, won a 1976 Urban Design Commission Award for Excellence and has delighted pedestrians and passersby ever since.

In 1997, Sara's dream of building a museum to honor her late hus-band to preserve the creations from his 60-year career as an artist in Georgia, came to fruition with the Steffen Thomas Museum of Art located in Buckhead, Georgia, near Madison. Steffan's style varied over the years, and some of his female forms have been compared to Matisse. But his work also has a distinctly cubist style, indicative of his early sculptor apprenticeship in Germany.

Address Peachtree Street & 15th Street NE, Atlanta, GA 30361, www.ocaatlanta.com/events/the-trilon-restoration | Getting there Red or Gold Line to Arts Center | Hours Unrestricted | Tip Inside Colony Square, behind Trilon Fountain, is the Goethe-Zentrum Atlanta/German Cultural Center, which hosts German language classes and movie nights, European wine tasting events, German soccer viewing events, and many other cultural events throughout the year (1201 Peachtree Street NE, www.german-institute.org).

100_Two-Headed Calf

Born in Georgia, immortalized under a golden dome

We've all heard about politicians talking out of both sides of their mouth, but the Georgia State Capitol Museum goes way beyond that to include polycephaly, the condition of being born with more than one head. Imagine if politicians really had two mouths! A popular Internet search: "Is the gold on the Georgia capitol dome real?" It is. And here's the connection: beneath that gold-gilded dome is an artifact you wouldn't believe unless you saw it: the taxidermied heads from a two-headed calf.

Soon after the Capitol Building opened, the position of state geologist was created, and that person was tasked with obtaining and displaying geological specimens to promote Georgia's natural resources. The ensuing museum, now located on the Capitol Building's fourth floor, evolved over the years to include taxidermy. Today, the Georgia Capitol Museum showcases the Capitol and Georgia government, but it also contains many artifacts from the original collection, including some oddities, like the two-headed calf that was born in the state, and also a two-headed snake, as well as other taxidermied animals found in Georgia, gems and minerals, folk art, and four large columns with Corinthian capitals showcasing the kinds of marbles mined in Georgia, including white Cherokee marble and Etowah pink marble. Also on display are the apron and elaborate collar John Davidson, Grand Master of Georgia Masons, wore when the cornerstone of the Capitol Building was placed on September 2, 1885.

The Georgia Capitol Building was renovated to look as it did when its doors first opened in 1889, including the wall colors and the light fixtures, which are exact replicas (today electric instead of gas-powered). Before the renovation, in 1977 the Georgia Capitol Building became a National Historic Landmark noted as "an outstanding structure, both architecturally and historically."

Address 206 Washington Street SW, Atlanta, GA 30304, +1 (404) 463-4536, www.libs.uga.edu/capitolmuseum/museum | Getting there Blue or Green Line to Georgia State | Hours Mon–Fri 8am–5pm | Tip The gold on the Georgia State Capitol Building's dome is indeed real! It comes from Dahlonega, Georgia. The Dahlonega Gold Museum Historic Site is a 70-minute drive north (1 Public Square, Dahlonega, www.gastateparks.org/DahlonegaGoldMuseum).

101 Union General Monument
They're not all Confederate monuments

Upon multiple square platforms of varying sizes in a pocket park in southeast Atlanta stands an erect cannon as a memorial to US Civil War Union soldier, Major General James Birdseye McPherson. The cannon stands without wheels, but its trunnions are intact. The memorial is enclosed by a fence made of eight cement posts and two rows of black metal poles. The top platform has *McPherson* engraved on the McPherson Avenue side, and there's an American flag mounted on the fence on the same side. McPherson graduated from the United States Military Academy at West Point and was commissioned into the Army Corps of Engineers, the same group that erected this monument.

There is a historical marker at the site, one side describing the circumstances of McPherson's death and the other side describes the eight-hour Battle of Atlanta. It also notes that two major generals were killed that day, McPherson and Confederate Major General William H. T. Walker, the namesake of Fort Walker – the last remaining breastworks in Atlanta, located in the southeastern corner of Grant Park. Twenty minutes away in East Point, Georgia, Fort McPherson was the namesake for Major General McPherson. The base was active from 1885 until 2011. Today, it's the site of movie-making magic: Tyler Perry Studios.

Refusing to surrender, McPherson was shot and killed on his way to William T. Sherman's headquarters while trying to escape capture by Confederate forces during the Battle of Atlanta on Friday, July 22, 1864. He was among more than 12,000 who perished that day, including more than 3,600 Union soldiers and nearly 8,500 Confederate soldiers. Confederate forces returned the body of McPherson to Union forces so that he could be given a proper burial.

Address 1415 McPherson Avenue SE, Atlanta, GA 30316 | **Getting there** Blue Line to Inman Park-Reynoldstown; bus 4 to Moreland Avenue SE and Faith Avenue SE | **Hours** Unrestricted | **Tip** You can see *The Battle of Atlanta*, one of only two cyclorama paintings in the country at the Atlanta History Center. This fully restored, 40-foot-tall painting is more than 130 years old (130 West Paces Ferry Road NW, www.atlantahistorycenter.com).

102 The Vortex

Home of the Quadruple Coronary Bypass Burger

The Vortex is largely considered to be the grandfather of burger culture in Atlanta. It was one of the first places to introduce high-quality burgers with unique twists well before it was trendy. You'll find a huge selection of beer, spirits and specialty cocktails, as well as ridiculously indulgent bar food. Oh, and this 21+ establishment is an official idiot-free zone! "Basically, every time an idiot would do something stupid, we'd add another rule to our list," says owner Michael Benoit.

Looking for entertainment? Just open the menu! Start with their Cheese Ball O'Glory or the Muthacluckin' Chicken Rolls. If you've never been here, you must not miss the burgers. Try the Fat Elvis, the Zombie Apocalypse, or the Ka'mana Wa'na Lei'ya. If your heart is set on a sandwich, enjoy the Yankee Ruben or the Big Naked Weenie. You're of legal drinking age, so enjoy a Hip-Mo-Tizer cocktail in a tiki mug in the shape of a laughing skull – just like the one you walked through to get inside! The mug is an additional cost or you can enjoy this rum libation in a regular cup, but what's the fun in that?

The Holy Grail of eating victories is winning their Superstack Challenge. The goal of the challenge is to finish eating an entire Quadruple Coronary Bypass Burger Meal within 30 minutes. The contents of the colossal meal include: one Quadruple Coronary Bypass Burger (it's massive!), 10 ounces of French fries, 10 ounces of tater tots, topped with sixteen ounces of the Vortex's own Cheesy-Cheese Goo, sprinkled with bacon bits, and two 32-ounce fountain soft drinks. And if you barf during the challenge, you get to clean it up. The entertainment level of this place is too deep to express in one chapter, but suffice it to say, if you want to enjoy damn good drinks and spectacular burgers in a grown-up-only, idiot-free atmosphere, this is the place for you!

Address 438 Moreland Avenue NE, Atlanta, GA 30307, +1 (404) 688-1828, www.thevortexatl.com | Getting there Bus 6 or 102 to Moreland Avenue and Euclid Avenue | Hours Sun–Thu 11am–midnight, Fri & Sat 11–2am | Tip Head to Laughing Skull Lounge (also 21+) at the Peachtree Street location of The Vortex. Some of the country's best comedic talent performs here, and Friday nights are "Atlanta's Best" (878 Peachtree Street NE, www.laughingskulllounge.com).

103 Waffle House Museum
The restaurant that launched a dining empire

"Scattered, smothered, and covered" is a phrase every Southerner knows well. It'd be a good bet that most Southerners have eaten at this nationally acclaimed dining destination that has served nearly 2,000,000,000 orders of hash browns. But there is only one Waffle House Museum.

It's located in the quaint Alpine village-esque town of Avondale Estates, part of Metro Atlanta and inside the perimeter ("ITP" as locals call it). The museum is available for tours by appointment only on Wednesdays at 11:30am or 1:30pm. To check for availability and schedule your tour, call them. This was the first Waffle House restaurant which opened in 1955 and launched a Southern dining empire. Today, there are more than 1,900 restaurants, all open 24 hours a day, 365 days per year since the very beginning, from Florida to New York to Colorado to Arizona.

The Waffle House Museum comprises two buildings, including the original restaurant, which features the dining room and the pantry, where food was stored, as well as prepared. Of note, in 1955, everything on the menu was made from scratch except for three items: Coca-Cola, Heinz ketchup, and Post Toasties cereal. The second, neighboring building houses numerous displays that include a restaurant counter, a jukebox, artifacts from Waffle Houses in New Orleans that fell to Hurricane Katrina, and countless other historical items that tell the story of an incredibly successful restaurant of more than 60 years.

There are recordings around the museum, so be sure to look for the activation buttons on the walls to hear stories that provide historical recollections and factoids. Interestingly, there were no tables in the original dining room. There was only the counter seating and a couple of benches against the opposing wall. The benches were for those guests who wanted only coffee, while the counter was reserved for dining guests.

Address 2719 East College Avenue, Decatur, GA 30030, +1 (770) 326-7086, www.wafflehouse.com/waffle-house-museum | Getting there Blue Line to Avondale Estates; bus 8 to East College Avenue and Sams Crossing | Hours See website for tour information | Tip Experience the real thing! There are dozens of Waffle House restaurants throughout Atlanta, but if you can't wait, head to the one four blocks east (2850 East College Avenue, Decatur, locations.wafflehouse.com).

104__ West Palisades Trail

Beautiful sights on an ancient river

The West Palisades Trail, part of a National Park Service National Recreation Area, is said to be among the most beautiful trails in Atlanta. Located in the northwest part of the city where the Chattahoochee River dips inside the Perimeter (or I-285, the interstate that fully circles Atlanta) and I-75. The Chattahoochee River was the dividing line between the Creek and Cherokee Nations, the Creeks dominating the south and east side of the river, and the Cherokee controlling the north and west side, which is where you'll find the West Palisades Trail. The name Chattahoochee is a Creek Indian word meaning "river of painted rocks."

If you're hiking the West Palisades Trail, know that it's a "moderate" lever, but only four miles long. You can bring your dog, but you must use a leash no longer than six feet. Bring your camera and visit year round for some spectacular views of the Chattahoochee River's changing foliage season by season. Most years, Atlanta has spectacular autumn foliage, but it lasts less time than you would experience in northern states. Spring also rings in a beautiful range of colors, as well as clustered dots of white from the many dogwood trees here. You'll see amazing views of the river as you meander, some featuring rock outcroppings, islands in the river, and you may even come across some wildlife along your route.

Wildlife is abundant in and around Atlanta. On this trail, you'll likely see herons, geese, and the occasional deer. Perhaps you may also see a river otter if you're lucky. If you do not see squirrels, something is terribly wrong – perhaps the zombie apocalypse is upon us. The fictional CDC headquarters from *The Walking Dead* is walking distance from here. The real CDC is 14 miles in the other direction. But all is well, and you will see plenty of squirrels. You'll also see a bamboo forest on the companion East Palisades Trail on the Creek Indian side.

Address 932 Akers Ridge Drive SE, Atlanta, GA 30339, www.atlantatrails.com/atlanta-hiking-trails | Getting there CobbLink bus 50 to Akers Mill Road and Akers Drive | Hours Dawn–dusk | Tip Find your way to the other side of the Chattahoochee River to explore the East Palisades Trail, where you can hike or bike and enjoy fantastic views (1425 Indian Trail NW, Sandy Springs, www.atlantatrails.com/trails-georgia).

105 Westview Cemetery
Home to some of Atlanta's finest

Today's Westview Cemetery opened in 1884 as an answer to Atlanta's running out of burial space. It was the city's first privately owned and operated cemetery, and has had more than 100,000 internments. At 582 acres, the cemetery continues to be active today, visited by families, friends, and tourists. With approximately 19 miles of roads on the property, you should download a map from the cemetery's website or have a GPS app available.

Numerous businesses have flourished around Westview, including Westview Floral Company, which provided florals for multiple dinners honoring President Grover Cleveland during his visit to Atlanta to see the 1895 Cotton States and International Exposition (see ch. 5) and to meet educator Booker T. Washington (see ch. 52).

The first "celebrity" interred at Westview was J. W. Pierce, a wealthy Texan, philanderer, and accidental celebrity for having been exhumed *three* different times after his accidental death. His wife in Texas told Westview that his body would be moved in the spring, but it never was. A few other notable graves at Westview include Asa Griggs Chandler, Jr., Coca-Cola founder and Atlanta mayor; Carling Dinkler, Sr., owner of Dinkler Plaza Hotel, where Martin Luther King, Jr. was honored for his Nobel Peace Prize in the South's first racially integrated banquet (see ch. 58); Adrien Esmilaire, circus entertainer billed as the world's smallest man at 27-inches tall, under 20 pounds, and known as "Little Mabb"; Henry W. Grady, *Atlanta Constitution* editor; William B. Hartsfield, Atlanta mayor and airport namesake; Alice J. Hawthorne, Centennial Olympic Park bombing victim; Ralph E. McGill, Pulitzer Prize winner and *Atlanta Constitution* editor; and Frederick W. Patterson, President Franklin D. Roosevelt's mortician. Learn the cemetery's extensive history in *Atlanta's Westview Cemetery* by local historian Jeff Clemmons.

Address Westview Drive at Ralph D. Abernathy Boulevard, Atlanta, GA 30310, +1 (404) 755-6611, www.westviewcemetery.com | Getting there Blue Line to West Lake | Hours Mon–Fri 9am–5:30pm, Sat 9:30am–2pm | Tip Just north of Atlanta is Marietta National Cemetery, where more than 10,000 Union soldiers found their final resting place (500 Washington Avenue, Marietta, www.cem.va.gov/cems/nchp/marietta.asp).

106 _ Winecoff Hotel Fire
Deadliest hotel fire ever leads to modern safety

Today's Ellis Hotel in the heart of Downtown Atlanta was built in 1913 and originally known as Winecoff Hotel, named for the hotel's builder, W. Frank Winecoff. The core construction of the 15-story, 195-room hotel was soundly built with fireproof material, and both operators and Atlanta officials considered the hotel to be "absolutely fireproof." Architects called it "…the latest thing in high-rise construction." Fire escapes were not included because it was thought that they would interfere with the exterior look of the building. Unvoiced was the knowledge that, while the core of the building was indeed fireproof, the contents were not. There was no fire detection system or sprinkler system.

On the fateful morning of Saturday, December 7, 1946, at approximately 3:00am, flames sparked what would be the deadliest hotel fire in American history. The flames quickly climbed the stairwell to the upper floors, and 119 of the nearly 300 guests perished in a fire, including 30 teenagers who were at a sponsored state youth conference. Mr. Winecoff, who had taken up residence in the hotel, also perished in the fire. Few of the victims died from burning, but rather asphyxiation by smoke and from jumping out of windows.

Arnold Hardy won the Pulitzer Prize for a photo of a woman who jumped from the burning building. Approximately 25 to 36 jumpers died, but the woman in the photo survived. She was identified as Daisy McCumber. This disaster was suspected to have started from a cigarette tossed into a mattress stored on a third-floor hallway. It became the catalyst for a number of improvements to building codes and forever altered the use of the term "fireproof" in construction.

What was one of Atlanta's tallest buildings at the time is today the Ellis Hotel, voted the #1 hotel in Atlanta by *Condé Nast Magazine* and is equipped with fire alarms and an automated sprinkler system.

Address 176 Peachtree Street NW, Atlanta, GA 30303, www.ellishotel.com | Getting there
Red Line to Peachtree Center | Hours Unrestricted from the outside only | Tip Fire Station
No. 11 was the first station to respond to the Winecoff Hotel fire. Today, the converted 1907
fire station is Negril Village, a Caribbean restaurant with elements honoring the building's
past (30 North Avenue NE, www.negrilvillageatl.com).

107 __ Woodrow Wilson's Office
New lawyer and future president chooses Atlanta

Woodrow Wilson moved to Atlanta in May of 1882 to open a law practice at 48 Marietta Street NW – before he had passed the bar. Fortunately, on October 19, 1882, he did pass the Georgia Bar Examination. He "hung out his shingle" – terminology of the day meaning to open a business – sharing an office with his business partner Edward Ireland Renick, also a former law student at the University of Virginia. Wilson was born in Staunton, Virginia, but grew up in Augusta, Georgia. He had dropped his first name (Thomas, or "Tommy") for the more distinguished "Woodrow."

Wilson wrote to a friend, "After innumerable hesitations as to a place of settlement, I have at length fixed upon Atlanta, Georgia. It more than any other Southern city offers all the advantages of business activity and enterprise… There appear to be no limits to the possibilities of her development; and I think to grow up with a new section is no small advantage to one who seeks to gain position and influence."

However, Wilson became discouraged and dismayed that Atlanta had not presented the opportunities he'd hoped. There were 143 attorneys in the city in 1883, not leaving many opportunities for young lawyers. So in June 1883, he enrolled at the Johns Hopkins University, where he earned a PhD, the only president to earn one. Thirty years after living in Atlanta, Woodrow Wilson would become the 28th President of the United States.

He was also the first US president of four to win a Nobel Peace Prize. Wilson died at his Washington, DC home on February 3, 1924, at age 67. He was buried in the Washington National Cathedral and is the only president whose final resting place is in the nation's capital. Atlanta held a memorial service for Wilson in the Atlanta Auditorium that thousands attended. While solemn in nature, there were spontaneous bursts of applause of appreciation during the speaker portion of the program.

Address 48 Marietta Street NW, Atlanta, GA 30303 (historic address, at the intersection of Marietta and Forsyth Streets) | Getting there Blue, Gold, Green, or Red Line to Five Points | Hours Unrestricted | Tip At the same intersection on Marietta Street is a bronze statue memorializing Atlanta's famous *New South* newspaper editor Henry W. Grady (Marietta Street NW at Forsyth Street NW, www.ocaatlanta.com/public_art/henry-w-grady).

108 World Athletes Monument

Where Atlanta mourned the death of Princess Diana

Commissioned by the Prince of Wales Foundation for Architecture, the World Athletes Monument, sometimes still called the Prince of Wales' Monument, was built for the 1996 Olympic Games as a "tribute to the athletes and spirit of international athletic competition." The monument was dedicated by Lord Morris, representing Queen Elizabeth II.

After the shocking death of Diana, Princess of Wales, the People's Princess, in 1997, Atlantans flocked to the World Athletes Monument, laying flowers and other mementos at its base. There were so many that traffic had to be diverted away from the monument. CNN reported an estimated 20,000 people went to the monument shortly after her passing. One of the artists of the World Athletes Monument was Martin Dawe, founder of Cherrylion Studios (see ch. 31) and the artist responsible for *Landing Gear* in Buckhead and a life-size bronze of President Franklin D. Roosevelt.

With five eight-foot-high Atlas figures atop a thirty-five-foot limestone base, it's not a monument that you're going to miss. And its solitary, triangular island home ensures a great view with no visual obstacles. In fact, there are quite a few fantastic backdrops, depending on where you're viewing it from. Instrumental in the overall project was Rodney Mims Cook, Jr., a descendant of two Atlanta Mayors, heavily involved in the Save the Fox campaign, and the leader of the Millennium Gate project at Atlantic Station. Cook has been described by some as "...a champion of beauty in the city of Atlanta." Now, Cook is working on a new park that will feature a statue of Indian chief Tomochichi.

The World Athletes Monument once again became a place of healing for the citizens of Atlanta. Many mourners placed small American flags here when President Ronald Reagan died in 2004.

Address 1409 Peachtree Street NW, Atlanta, GA 30309 | Getting there Red or Gold Line to Arts Center | Hours Unrestricted | Tip Keep the cultural conversation going back down on West Peachtree Street at the trendy Studio Bar & Cocktail Garden at Artmore Hotel (1302 West Peachtree Street, www.artmorehotel.com).

109 World War I Memorial

Honoring Fulton County's fallen heroes

This World War I memorial is hiding in plain sight in Pershing Point Park, a tiny spot on busy Peachtree Street in the business district of Midtown Atlanta. Placed by the War Mother's Service Star Legion in 1920, the memorial is dedicated to Georgians who perished in WWI. A marble plaque with the dedication is the focal point, with a knee-high wall stretching behind the memorial that lists the names of the fallen soldiers from Georgia's Fulton County, one of the three counties in Atlanta's city limits. In conjunction with the 100th anniversary of the start of World War I, the neighboring Atlanta office of the Jones Day law firm sponsored the rededication of the recently restored memorial.

There were more military training camps in Georgia than any other state in the country, from which more than 100,000 men and women joined the war effort. The names listed on the memorial are in alphabetical order by last name, categorized by job distinction, including Infantry (the highest number lost), Cavalry, Engineers, and Aviation.

The sole woman listed is a civilian, a Miss Camille O'Brien, a Red Cross nurse. She was a member of the Emory Unit and was the only Red Cross nurse from Atlanta. When her unit was recalled, she heroically remained behind to tend to wounded soldiers. She died of spinal meningitis in 1919, and was laid to rest in Atlanta's Greenwood Cemetery. The plaque calls them all "fallen heroes." Look for the "Negroes" section that includes the names of African-American souls lost in the Infantry, Machine Gun, Navy, and Labor Corps job distinctions.

Pershing Point Park is named for Gen. John Joseph "Black Jack" Pershing (1860–1948). His most famous post was serving as commander of the American Expeditionary Forces (AEF) on the Western Front in World War I. Pershing attained the rank of General of the Armies, the highest post in the US Army.

110 Wren's Nest
A presidential owl

During a 1906 visit to Atlanta, President Theodore Roosevelt said of Joel Chandler Harris, "Presidents may come and presidents may go, but Uncle Remus stays put. Georgia has done a great many things for the Union, but she has never done more than when she gave Joel Chandler Harris to American literature."

Best known for giving a voice to African-American folklore through his *Uncle Remus and Brer Rabbit* stories, Harris was born December 1845 and raised in Eatonton, Georgia. Later in Harris' life, he and President Roosevelt would become friends and visit each other's homes. The Harris' home was known as Wren's Nest, and Roosevelt would stop by to visit. Look for the taxidermied owl in the music room, a gift from Roosevelt himself. The president also wrote letters to Harris, sometimes sharing lively accounts of his own menagerie living at the White House.

The Wren's Nest got its name from an actual wren's nest. In 1900, two birds built their nest in the Harris' mailbox. A second mailbox was erected so as not to disturb the new residents, but the newly built mailbox quickly became home to even more wrens. The name "Wren's Nest" was soon adopted as the name of the house and it stuck. The original mailbox is on display in the home.

Already a nice home, Harris added a distinctive Queen Anne Victorian-style exterior. It's one of the few remaining examples of this style home still standing in Atlanta. Mr. Harris' bedroom is roped off, remaining nearly exactly as it was in 1908 when he passed away. The room is not accessible directly, but you can see it perfectly from the hallway. At the time of this writing, another room is being pre-pared for temporary exhibits. When Harris moved in, he had just published his first *Uncle Remus* book and would write the significant portion of the total 194 stories while sitting on the front porch of the Wren's Nest.

Address 1050 Ralph David Abernathy Boulevard SW, Atlanta, GA 30310, +1 (404) 753-7735, www.wrensnestonline.com | Getting there Red Line to West End; bus 71 to Ralph David Abernathy Boulevard SW and Lawton Street SW | Hours Sat 10am–4pm, Sun noon–4pm, Mon–Fri by appointment only | Tip Since its founding in 1887, the Piedmont Driving Club has enjoyed a reputation as one of the most prestigious private clubs in the South. President Roosevelt visited here as well. Drive past or visit during the Phoenix Flies program (1215 Piedmont Avenue NE, www.drivingclub.org).

111 Zoo Atlanta's Origins
From bankrupt circus to high-tech habitats

Open more days than any other major attraction in Atlanta – 363 days per year, closed only on Thanksgiving and Christmas – Zoo Atlanta has an interesting origin story. A traveling circus in 1889, with a menagerie of "exotic" animals, went bankrupt while on an Atlanta stopover. A local businessman purchased the collection of animals and donated them to the City of Atlanta. The city decided to give them a new home in Grant Park, thus creating Zoo Atlanta, where it remains today, entertaining and educating generation after generation. Grant Park is also Atlanta's oldest surviving park.

The origins of Zoo Atlanta also included numerous donations from Coca-Cola founder Asa Candler's private animal collection, which he kept at his home, the walled Briarcliff Manor. Having received numerous complaints from neighbors about his menagerie, the newly founded public zoo happily took in his animals, too. Among Candler's collection were two elephants named "Coca" and "Cola." Today, Zoo Atlanta's 40-acre site is home to approximately 1,500 animals, representing 220 species. Visit – if you dare – the new, high-tech reptile house, fondly named "Scaly Slimy Spectacular," a new $18 million complex that offers a state-of-the art digital and interactive experience, including touch screens with images and videos for greater learning and understanding of the more than 70 species there.

Today the zoo's conservation efforts span the reach of the globe with giant pandas on loan from China (check out the website's PandaCam), to African elephants, and a host of other endangered or at-risk species.

The zoo rests on land donated to the city by Lemuel P. Grant in 1881, the park's namesake. The African Savanna habitat was expanded after the zoo acquired the neighboring property – get close to elephants, giraffes, zebras, and meerkats!

Address 800 Cherokee Avenue SE, Atlanta, GA 30315, +1 (404) 624-9453,
www.zooatlanta.org | Getting there Bus 832 to Cherokee Avenue | Hours Daily
9:30am–5:30pm | Tip Visit the nearby L. P. Grant Mansion, which originally held
600 acres of land. It's also the birthplace of golf legend Bobby Jones (see ch. 41).
Today, it's the Atlanta Preservation Center's headquarters (327 Saint Paul Avenue SE,
www.atlantapreservationcenter.com).

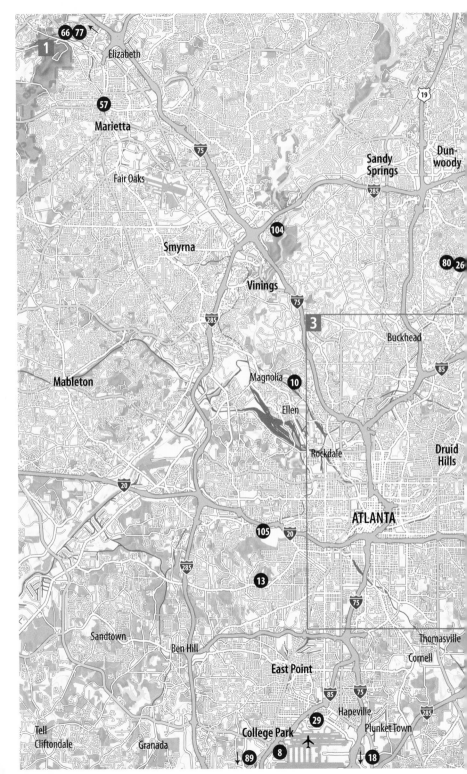

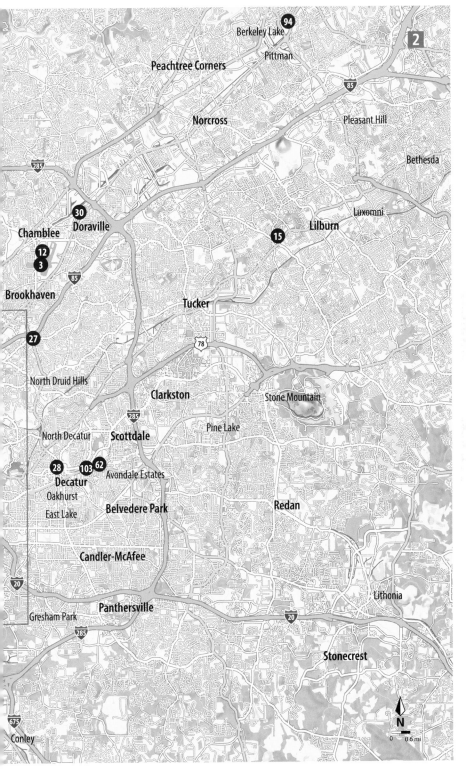

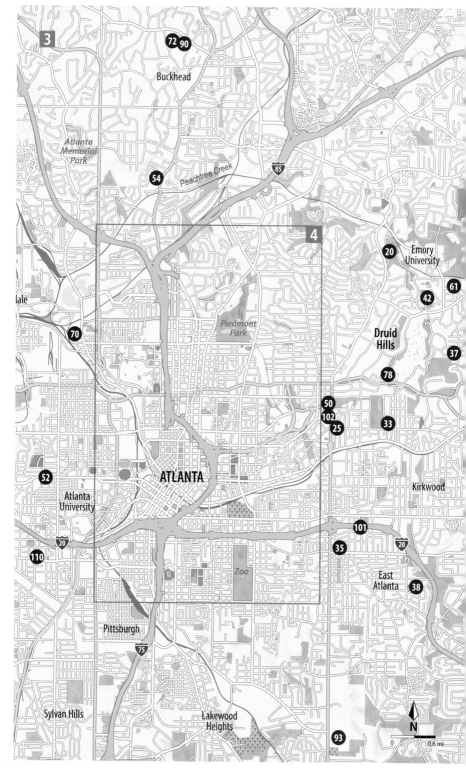

3

72 90

Buckhead

Atlanta
Memorial
Park

54

Peachtree Creek

85

4

20

Emory
University

61

42

70

Piedmont
Park

Druid
Hills

37

78

50

102

25

33

52

ATLANTA

Kirkwood

Atlanta
University

20

110

101

35

20

Zoo

East
Atlanta

38

Pittsburgh

75

Sylvan Hills

Lakewood
Heights

93

N

0   0.6 mi

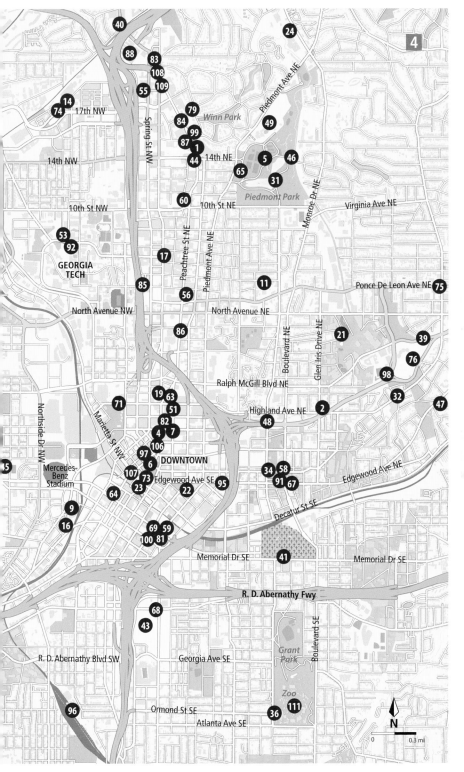

Kelsey Roslin, Nick Yeager,
Jesse Pitzler
**111 Places in Austin
That You Must Not Miss**
ISBN 978-3-7408-0748-1

Katrina Nattress, Jason Quigley
**111 Places in Portland
That You Must Not Miss**
ISBN 978-3-7408-0750-4

Floriana Petersen, Steve Werney
**111 Places in Silicon Valley
That You Must Not Miss**
ISBN 978-3-7408-0493-0

Floriana Petersen, Steve Werney
**111 Places in San Francisco
That You Must Not Miss**
ISBN 978-3-95451-609-4

Amy Bizzarri, Susie Inverso
**111 Places in Chicago
That You Must Not Miss**
ISBN 978-3-7408-0156-4

Michelle Madden, Janet McMillan
**111 Places in Milwaukee
That You Must Not Miss**
ISBN 978-3-7408-0491-6

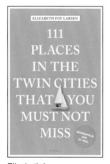

Elisabeth Larsen
**111 Places in the Twin Cities
That You Must Not Miss**
ISBN 978-3-7408-0029-1

Sandra Gurvis, Mitch Geiser
**111 Places in Columbus
That You Must Not Miss**
ISBN 978-3-7408-0600-2

Jo-Anne Elikann
**111 Places in New York
That You Must Not Miss**
ISBN 978-3-95451-052-8

Wendy Lubovich, Jean Hodgens
111 Places in the Hamptons
That You Must Not Miss
ISBN 978-3-7408-0751-1

Wendy Lubovich, Ed Lefkowicz
111 Museums in New York
That You Must Not Miss
ISBN 978-3-7408-0379-7

Leslie Adatto, Clay Williams
111 Rooftops in New York
That You Must Not Miss
ISBN 978-3-7408-0495-4

John Major, Ed Lefkowicz
111 Places in Brooklyn
That You Must Not Miss
ISBN 978-3-7408-0380-3

Kevin C. Fitzpatrick, Joe Conzo
111 Places in the Bronx
That You Must Not Miss
ISBN 978-3-7408-0492-3

Joe DiStefano, Clay Williams
111 Places in Queens
That You Must Not Miss
ISBN 978-3-7408-0020-8

Andréa Seiger, John Dean
111 Places in Washington
That You Must Not Miss
ISBN 978-3-7408-0258-5

Dave Doroghy, Graeme Menzies
111 Places in Vancouver
That You Must Not Miss
ISBN 978-3-7408-0494-7

Anita Mai Genua,
Clare Davenport,
Elizabeth Lenell Davies
111 Places in Toronto
That You Must Not Miss
ISBN 978-3-7408-0257-8

I'm deeply grateful to Emons Publishing for taking a chance on this first-time author and for inviting me to photograph the book, too – that made this an incredibly special experience. A huge "Thank you!" to my wonderful editor Karen Seiger who has always been there for me, guided me, helped me, encouraged me, not only listened but heard me, and I love that we shared so many laughs together. I feel like I've made a new lifelong friend. I owe this amazing opportunity to Chef Virginia Willis. Thank you, Virginia, for recommending me to Emons!

Thank you, thank you, thank you to my friend Barry Holland for years and years of wandering throughout Metro Atlanta and beyond, not always knowing what you were getting yourself into, but always making the adventure fun and memorable. Nikki Griffin, thank you for all the foodie, restaurant, and brewery experiences, as well as the sci-fi conventions. To Lisa and Jeff Adler, and Ryan Olivetti, thank you for fueling my love of theatre and making me feel like a part of Atlanta's theatre community. Patti Davis and Carrie Burns, I'm eternally grateful to you for sharing and showing me parts of Atlanta that I might never have discovered otherwise, but I'm especially thankful for your friendship. For your support, encouragement, and friendship when I was a budding blogger, thank you to Sue Rodman, Lesli Peterson, Beth Clark, and Terry Kearns. Each of you welcomed me to the Atlanta blogging community with open arms – I'll always be grateful for that.

Last, but certainly not least, thank you to the Atlanta History Center's Kenan Research Center, where I spent many hours, especially in the beginning, researching their fascinating collections and libraries. The staff was consistently courteous and helpful. Thank you to friends, fans, and everyone who has enthusiastically supported this project, you made the experience absolutely amazing!

Travis Swann Taylor, writing since he could wield a pen, has an ever-growing sense of wanderlust and seeks out stories from around the world. A self-taught photographer, he has carried a camera since the age of 10. Travis chose Atlanta to call his home, and today, he continues to find awe and fascination throughout the city.